AL AYOUN
JORDAN

DI TAYLOR & **TONY HOWARD**

OTHER BOOKS BY
TONY HOWARD & DI TAYLOR

Treks and Climbs in Wadi Rum, Jordan *Cicerone Press*
Jordan – Walks, Treks, Caves, Climbs & Canyons *Cicerone Press*
Walks in Palestine and The Nativity Trail *Cicerone Press*
Climbs, Scrambles & Walks in Romsdal *Cordee*
Troll Wall *Vertebrate Publishing*

WALKS, TREKS, CLIMBS & CAVES IN AL AYOUN, JORDAN
By Di Taylor & Tony Howard
First edition 2011
Copyright © Di Taylor & Tony Howard 2011

Maps & photos by the authors

Front cover photo: Approaching Judeita, Route 12, the Judeita Trail
Back cover photo: Climbing *The First Taste* at Al Warda al Hamra, Rasoun in the background

ISBN 978-1-906148-34-8

Printed & bound by *National Press* in The Hashemite Kingdom of Jordan

 Design & production by Jane Beagley
www.v-graphics.co.uk

PERMISSIONS
We thank the following copyright holder for permission to quote from her book:
Wingbeat Publishing Ltd. *Kernow, A Land Apart.* 2002, Deborah King

ADVICE TO READERS
The authors and publisher cannot accept any responsibility for loss, injury or inconvenience arising from the use of information contained in this guide. Readers are advised that whilst every effort is taken by the authors to ensure the accuracy of this guidebook, changes can and do occur which may affect it. It is advisable to check locally on transport, accommodation, shops etc. Also please be aware that paths may alter or be eradicated by road-building, landslip, flash-floods (not infrequent in narrow valleys) or even change of ownership. The publisher and authors would welcome notes of any changes.

Contents

Thanks to all concerned

...in the context of an ever-warming world, if we continue to fly for our pleasure and education, we need to ensure that such tourism is not itself damaging, and that it genuinely benefits the host communities at the other end.

Chris Brazier, New Internationalist, March 2008

In spring 2009, we were invited to assess the potential of the Ayoun area for climbing and trekking in order that the Ayoun community might benefit from adventure tourism. We returned in spring 2010 and 2011 to complete our part of the project and have had a wonderful time in the area. We would like to thank the following for making our visits so enjoyable and successful and hope this guide will be some reward for the enthusiasm, friendship and hospitality given to us by the people of Al Ayoun.

Daniel Adamson and William Ury, for their initial invitation and support.

Ramez Habash and Suhair Ismail for facilitating our work in Al Ayoun.

Mohammed abu Ibrahim, then Mayor of Al Ayoun, now Tourism Coordinator, for his encouragement and support.

Mahmoud Hawawreh and Eisa Dweekat, local guides and residents of Al Ayoun, for the pleasure of their company on some of the walks and for their exemplary hospitality.

Al Ayoun Society/Orjan for representing the Orjan community.

Mark and Julie Khano of Sarha, also their children, Haneen and Gabriel, for their hospitality in Amman and for the pleasure of their company on some of the walks and climbs.

Brian and Andjelka Hodgkinson for their hospitality in Amman and for Brian's good company in the hills.

Mick Shaw, lifetime companion in the mountains and regular n.o.m.a.d.s. team member for joining us on some of the climbs, even on the rainiest day of spring 2009!

Revd Andrew Ashdown of Wider Horizons (our companion and mentor on the Nativity Trail in Palestine) and his wife Victoria, for advice on the Christian aspects of some of Al Ayoun's archaeological sites.

Jon Barton, John Coefield and Jane Beagley of Vertebrate Graphics for supporting this project, fitting it into their schedule on short notice and creating such a good looking book. Nisreen Zait of the Jordan Bookcentre for her helpful advice.

The staff of the Natural History Museum, UK, for help with flower identification.

Dick Simon for his help in locating a sponsor for publishing the guide.

Hazem Malhas and Jane Taylor for facilitating the sponsorship, and also for Jane's help with locating the National Press printers in The Hashemite Kingdom of Jordan, and working with them on this book.

And finally, a very special thanks to Fadi Ghandour for his generous sponsorship of the book in cooperation with Al Ayoun Society, without which it could never have been published.

Di Taylor and Tony Howard
August 2011

ᑔ.o.ᗰ.ᗩ.ᑔ.s.

NEW OPPORTUNITIES FOR
MOUNTAINEERING, ADVENTURE
AND DESERT SPORTS

Dedication

DESCENDING THROUGH PINES NEAR ASHRAFIEH ON THE TREK TO PELLA, ROUTE 14

A dream you dream alone is only a dream.
A dream you dream together is a reality.

John Lennon

To the people of Al Ayoun, also to all those in Jordan
who continue to inspire and assist us in our explorations.

"There is much profit to be derived from seeing new lands
and new houses, in seeing beautiful gardens and fields,
in seeing different faces and coming across different
languages and colours, and in witnessing the wonders of
different countries. The peace that one finds under the
shade of large trees is unparalleled. Eating in the mosques,
drinking from streams, and sleeping wherever one finds
a place when night comes, these all instil affability and
humbleness in a person. The traveller befriends all those
whom he loves for Allah's sake and he has no reason to
flatter or to be artificial. Add to these benefits all of the
happiness that the traveller's heart feels when he reaches
his destination, and the thrill he experiences after having
overcome all of the obstacles that were on his way.
If those who are averse to leaving their homelands knew
all of this, they would learn that all of the individual
pleasures of the world are combined in the noble pursuit
of travelling. There is nothing more enjoyable to a
traveller than the beautiful sights and the wonderful
activities that are part of travelling through Allah's wide
earth. And the non-traveller is deprived of all of this."

The Noble Scholar of Hadeeth, Ramhumuzi
Source: *Don't be Sad, Sheikh 'Aaidh ibn Abdullah al-Qarni, 2003*

Welcome to Al Ayoun

RARE SCILLA HYACINTHOIDES, AL AYOUN

> **Anyone who claims there is nothing left to explore lacks imagination.**
>
> *Felicity Aston, Geographical Magazine, 2008*

Since we first visited Jordan in 1984, discovering the climbing and trekking potential of Wadi Rum, Jordan has continued to play a major role in our lives; the warm welcome, the hot sun, and the promise of new areas to explore are always irresistible after a grey English winter. It was therefore with real pleasure that we received an invite from Daniel Adamson in 2009 to join him in Al Ayoun, now one of our favourite parts of the Kingdom, especially in spring, to help develop the area for the benefit of the local community by searching out new treks and climbs.

Daniel and the local people had already developed the Ayoun Trail as part of the Abraham's Path (*Masar Ibrahim al Khalil*), a route of walking and cultural tourism based on the journeys of Abraham or Ibrahim through the Middle East. The story is a four thousand year old spiritual tradition shared by more than three billion people. Walking the Ayoun Trail and other routes, or coming to the area to climb and explore, provides opportunities for meeting and connection for people of all faiths and cultures, inviting us to remember our common origins, to respect our cultural differences, and to recognize our shared humanity. It also brings economic benefits to the Al Ayoun community who now run the project. See **www.abrahampath.org** for further info.

For us, meeting and spending time with the people of Al Ayoun was a wonderful experience and we hope that the routes described in this book will attract others to this uniquely beautiful rural area. We certainly recommend it – maybe we will see you there, as we will, for sure, continue to return.

Di Taylor and Tony Howard
August 2011

THE BLACK IRIS, JORDAN'S NATIONAL FLOWER, AL AYOUN

The members of Al Ayoun Cooperative Society would like to welcome you to our villages and beautiful valleys and hills. Whether you are walkers or climbers or maybe coming to explore caves or to enjoy the spring-time flowers or simply to relax, we are happy to be your hosts. Our homes are open for you to enjoy a homestay and experience our wonderful home-cooked food grown in our orchards and fields or gathered wild from the hills. You are our guests and we are ready to help in any way. Do not hesitate to ask.
Ahlan wa Sahlan.

Dr Ramzi Tabbalat
Al Ayoun Society Hon President

أهلا وسهلا بكم في العيون

يسر رئيس وأعضاء جمعية العيون التعاونية ان يرحبوا بك
ضيفا في قرانا ووديانا وجبالنا الجميلة. وسواء كنت من
هواة المشى أو التسلق أو كنت من هواة اكتشاف الكهوف
أو ممن يحبون التمتع بأزهار الربيع والا سترخاء بين أحضان
الطبيعة فنحن هنا نسعد باستضافتك. بيوتنا مفتوحة لك
لقضاء ليلة أو أكثر نقدم لك خلا لها أشهى أطباق الطعام المعد
منزليا من منتجات حقولنا وما ينبت حولها على سفوح
الجبال وفي بطون الأ ودية. أنت ضيفنا الغالي ولن نتردد
لحظة في خدمتك أو الا ستجابة لمطالبك ورغباتك. فأهلا وسهلا .

الرئيس الفخري لجمعية العيون التعاونية الدكتور رمزي طبلت

Introduction

The middle country... between the Yarmuk and the Jabbok (Zarqa River), has its ridges covered by forests, under which you may march for the whole day in breezy and fragrant shade; the valleys hold orchards of pomegranate, apricot and olive, there are many vineyards, on the open fields are plains of wheat and maize, and the few moors are rich in fragrant herbs... perfume and medicine for the whole Eastern world.

The Historical Geography of the Holy Land, George Adam-Smith DD, 1894

Al Ayoun is one of the most beautiful and verdant regions in the Kingdom – more so than any other part of Jordan; its Mediterranean climate has enabled the cultivation of vines, olives, figs, pomegranates, wheat and other crops. Its deep valleys shelter forests of evergreen oak, Palestinian pistachio, carob and wild Syrian pear, often entangled in honeysuckle, prickly ivy, thorny burnet, rock rose and joint-pine; the Palestinian buckthorn, the sensually smooth, red-barked strawberry tree and the Judas tree, which bears flowers directly on its trunk, also grow here, whilst high above, Aleppo pines and Palestinian evergreen oaks cast their welcome shade for shepherds and their flocks on hillsides where streams flow from perennial springs.

Due to the area's plentiful water supply, man has lived here since prehistoric times, perhaps most notably at Pella, but our ancestors have left dolmens and other signs of their passage over the millennia in and around most of Al Ayoun's villages. The ancient olive trees, some of them five metres in girth, are famous in Jordan and said to date from Roman times – the local people proudly claim their olive oil is the best in the country. The community is also amongst the most generous and hospitable that a traveller could hope to find, for the most part living a quiet rural life, tolerant and understanding of other religions and customs.

The three main villages

The area is known throughout Jordan for the quality of its olive oil and fruit: fig, pomegranate, carob, cherry, plum and quince as well as almonds grow here,

ANCIENT OLIVE TREE, ORJAN, ROUTE 12, THE JUDEITA TRAIL

nurtured by spring-fed irrigation channels, which were once used to power water mills on their way down the valley. Its three villages, Rasoun, Orjan and Baoun are hidden in the hills above the upper reaches of Wadi Yabis, immediately north of Ajloun and only an hour from Amman yet in a quiet landscape of olive groves, orchards and terraced fields, of farming and herding where rural values, traditions and customs are still important, where food is served with justifiable pride together with bread, freshly baked in a clay *taboon* oven and aromatic herbs, locally grown or gathered wild from the hills.

Heading east to west down the valley, the village of Rasoun lies near the source of the springs. In addition to its agriculture, it is also the location of the Soap House producing hand-made soaps from local olive oil and herbs, an innovative rural development project of Jordan's Royal Society for the Conservation of Nature (RSCN) whose nearby Ajloun Forest Reserve is in the hills above. It was also chosen by the RSCN for the location of its new Calligraphy Centre where visitors can have

their names and favourite phrases finely written in Arabic on T-shirts and pieces of leather, cloth or silk. Rasoun also has a ruined church, its font still visible, whilst Bronze Age dolmens and other megalithic graves dating back 5000 years or more are found on the surrounding hills. There is now a campsite here run by local people.

Downstream, across the river from Orjan, a small farm, around which hives and pigeon cotes dot the hillside, sells jam and honey for which the region is also famous. Across the river, below the village, the RSCN have opened their Biscuit House, which, as well as making and selling biscuits, is also an eco-lodge. The cave dwellings of a 4th to 6th century cliff hermitage are nearby, and there is still a small Christian community above Orjan, at Ras ed Deir. A lodge and campsite is also proposed in the area.

The third village is Baoun, adjacent to which are the hilltop Roman ruins of Ras al Qasr, or Castle Head, where there is believed to be buried treasure, which, the locals say, has given the village its name, Baoun being derived from *Maoun*

FIG TREES, WADI ORJAN, ROUTE 12, THE JUDEITA TRAIL

el Dhahab or Pot of Gold. It was here that Aisha bint Ahmad al Baouni was born, renowned in her own lifetime as a Sufi theologian, mystic, poet and calligrapher who preached in the great centres of Cairo and Damascus, where she died in 1516. Recognised as the finest female scholar of her era, and acknowledged by UNESCO for her contribution to Islamic civilisation, a Cultural Forum has been established in her name in the village.

A wealth of history

In addition to the three main villages described above, other neighbouring villages also have their own places of interest and are connected to Al Ayoun by treks or by pleasant drives on generally quiet country lanes. The great 14th century Moroccan traveller Abu 'Abdallah ibn Battuta, passed though the region in July 1326 on his way from Cairo via Nablus and the Golan Heights to Damascus, to join the Hajj to Mecca and would have been aware of the ancient history of the region, particularly of Pella, one of the oldest archaeological sites in Jordan,

in the Jordan Valley below Al Ayoun: there has been human activity there for almost a million years, the Greeks and Romans in particular leaving their mark in the first and second centuries BC.

In nearby Wadi abu Salih, there are Iron Age dolmens close to the trek down from Ashrafieh where columns said to be from the Greek Temple of Dion can be found. Also above Pella are the ruins of a Byzantine church with well-preserved mosaics, close to the *Kahf el Messih* – the 'Jesus Cave' where, according to local legend, Jesus stayed around the time of his baptism in the River Jordan by John the Baptist. Although a visit by Jesus to the Pella area is not specifically attested in the Bible, it was an important city on the route to Galilee and one of the 'towns of the Decapolis' that Jesus very likely visited and preached in. It would also make sense that Jesus would have passed through Pella on his way to or from his baptism at 'Bethany beyond the Jordan' as Pella was a major town en route.

The remains of another Byzantine church can be found in Zubia, in a part of the

THE RUINED PALACE OF AL'ALI SHREIDAH, TIBNA

village known as *ed deir*, 'the monastery', where there are also ancient houses and stables. The nearby village of Tibna, high on a mountain ridge, is the location of the splendid two-storey home built for the Ottoman governor of the region, known as Al'ali Shreidah; here also is the Zeidani mosque and a *majlis* or meeting hall built in 1750AD. Ain Zubia, a spring in the valley between Zubia and Tibna served as a major source of water for these and other settlements including Khirbet 'Us 'us of which little now remains other than ancient underground water cisterns whilst the ruins of Qabla with its huge carved water cisterns hide in the woods at the head of the valley, both sites being reputedly of Roman origin.

The most remarkable of Al Ayoun's Byzantine church ruins, Mar Elyas, has been a sacred place since remote antiquity. The present church was built somewhere in the first decades of the 7th century BC, just after the devastating invasion of the Persian armies and just before the coming of Islam to Jordan. The surviving mosaics show flower motifs and bold abstract designs, showing how Byzantine geometry influenced the development of Islamic art. Discovered in 1999, Mar Elyas is situated high on a hilltop above the village of Baoun. It is associated with the Prophet Elijah, as is the ruined Mameluke mosque at Listib on the adjacent hilltop, which may have been inhabited since Hellenistic times. The Qu'ran calls Elijah "an honourable man" and "a messenger" (6:86; 37:123), and says "we left mention of him among later men" (37:130), referring to Elijah's association with John the Baptist and Jesus. The Vatican named the area a pilgrimage destination in 2000.

Below Mar Elyas the villages of Al Ayoun are an easy walk to the north. Thirty kilometres further north, but hidden from view are the Greco-Roman ruins of Um Qais, ancient Gadara, another of the towns of the Decapolis and traditionally the place where some demon-possessed men begged Jesus to send their evil spirits into some nearby pigs, whereupon the herd rushed down to Lake Galilee and were drowned. (Matthew 8:28–34; Mark 5: 1–20; Luke 8: 26–30.)

Down to the west of Baoun, below Kufr Abil, Wadi Yabis flows from ancient 'Roman' olive groves through a limestone gorge and arid hills, the location of dolmens and Palaeolithic caves, to the Jordan Valley, which is two hundred metres below sea level at this point, despite being around 400 kilometres north of the Red Sea. Further west, the hills of Palestine and the pyramidal, extinct volcanic cinder cone of Mt Tabor, regarded by Christians as the 'Mount of Transfiguration', are visible in the distance, whilst the Islamic hilltop fortress of Ajloun stands proudly on its summit not far to the south and concealed beyond is the great Roman city of Jerash.

CHILDREN ENJOYING THE WATER AT THE OUDEH WATER MILL

Oh guest, should you visit us, you would find us the guests
and you the Master of the House.

From Al Mostatraf, 14th century Islamic treatise on living by Al Absheehi

A warm welcome

The first walk to be opened in the area
was the *Darb al Ayoun*, or Al Ayoun Trail,
which begins in Rasoun and ends at the
hilltop of Tel Mar Elyas. This route,
together with its developing network of
host families and local guides, has been
created by the people of Al Ayoun as the
first stage of a drive to bring more visitors
to this unspoilt part of Jordan. It now forms
the centrepiece of the network of trails,
climbs and caves described in this book,
inviting visitors to explore the beautiful
landscape and to meet and spend time with
the hospitable people. The idea behind this
ambitious endeavour is to create a place
of meeting and connection for people of
all faiths and cultures, as well as to open
economic opportunities based on eco-
tourism in Al Ayoun and neighbouring
rural communities.

The emphasis on villages and hospitality
– meeting the people rather than escaping
into the wilderness – is at the heart of the

LOCAL FARMER STOPS FOR A CHAT, ROUTES 9 AND 14, WADI ABU SALIH TO PELLA

> **The Chief takes less than he is given**
> **And gives more than he has taken.**
>
> *Sufi, Kitab-i-Ami Daria*

project, though the final route in this book, through the forest and gorges of Sirin, will gave you a taste of the latter. The other walks described here will take you from the villages of Al Ayoun, past the springs, the ancient groves and orchards, the dolmens, churches and mosques, even as far as Greco-Roman Pella in the Jordan Valley.

You will be able to explore sites spanning five millennia, and experience the variety and beauty of the area with its eco-systems ranging from the Mediterranean hill climate down to the sub-tropical Jordan Valley, supporting a diversity of birdlife such as the turtle dove, hooded crow, goldfinch, great tit, jay, Palestinian Sunbird, and even eagles and buzzards; other birds including cranes and raptors pass by on their bi-annual migrations along the Jordan Valley. You may also see wildlife (or signs of wildlife) including tortoises, foxes, badgers, snakes, wild boars and even wolves.

Finally, and maybe most memorably, you will have the opportunity to spend time with the people who live and work in Al Ayoun, perhaps even enjoying a home-stay and the superb local food, which is central to the whole Al Ayoun experience – an expression of the landscape and culture – what more could you want!

Culture & environment matters

These notes are based on '*A Third World Stopover – The Tourism Debate*' by Ron O'Grady:

- Travel in a spirit of humility and with a desire to learn about the people of your host country.
- Be sensitively aware of the feelings of other people. This applies very much to photography – do not take photographs of people without first asking for their permission.

AL AYOUN HOSPITALITY

Introduction

The true servants of the most gracious are those who tread gently on the earth.

The Qu'ran. Sura 25, verse 63

- Cultivate the habit of asking questions, listening, observing and learning.
- Realise other people's time concepts and thought patterns may differ from your own.
- Discover the enrichment of seeing a different way of life, through other eyes.
- Acquaint yourself with local customs. What is courteous in one country may be quite the reverse in another.
- Do not make promises to people in your host country such as sending photos when you get home unless you intend to carry them through.
- An extravagant display of wealth is insensitive to local people who may have much less than you. Nevertheless, respect and accept genuinely given hospitality – do not taint your hosts by offering money when none is required but discreetly establish first what is expected.

Now, moving on to environmental concerns. Below is an amalgam of the International Union of Alpine Associations (UIAA) Mountain Code, The British Mountaineering Council's conservation booklet – Tread Lightly, and the Himalayan Tourist Code published by Tourism Concern.

- Make no open fires and discourage others from doing so on your behalf unless it is clearly safe to do so and dead wood is plentiful.
- Remove litter, burn or bury paper and carry out all non-degradable litter. Keep campsites clean.
- Graffiti are permanent examples of environmental pollution.
- Avoid using pollutants such as detergents in streams, wells or springs. If no toilet facilities are available, make sure you go far away from water sources, and bury waste. Burn toilet paper or use water instead.
- Do not disturb nesting birds or other wildlife and respect sites of geological, archaeological or other scientific interest. Plants should be left to flourish in their natural environment.
- Do not disturb livestock or damage walls, crops or vegetation.
- Avoid causing unnecessary erosion (such as taking shortcuts on footpaths). Wear lightweight boots or trainers and tread carefully, especially in descent. Do not leave unnecessary waymarks.
- Rock climbers should respect established mountain traditions in ethical matters such as the use of chalk, pitons or bolts etc. Avoid indiscriminate or excessive use of fixed equipment.
- Cavers should respect the delicate cave environment, flora and fauna.
- Help your guides and porters to follow conservation measures.

Maps & equipment

There is a 1:50,000 map series to Jordan in English (code K737) dating from the 1960s and '70s, and a new series in Arabic to the same scale, but they are almost impossible to obtain.

If you want to try, contact:

The Royal Geographical Centre

PO Box 20214, 11118 Amman
T 009626 5345188
E rjgc@rjgc.gov.jo
www.rjgc.gov.jo

Hopefully the maps in this guide will be adequate although hiring a local guide with knowledge of the area is always worth doing and a GPS will be useful as GPS points are given in the route descriptions. It should be possible to do all the walks in this book without specialist equipment or help but a compass is always useful and water and a small first aid kit are essentials, as usually are sun hat, sun glasses and cream, though in winter and spring you may need waterproofs. It can even snow on the hills. Whatever the weather you should dress with respect for the local culture.

For the more complex treks, route finding skills will inevitably be needed due to the small scale of the maps and consequent limited information. In particular the 'contour' lines are there to give an idea of the general inclination of the land rather than to accurately define any specific altitude, though approximate maximum and minimum heights are shown. The scale also is approximate.

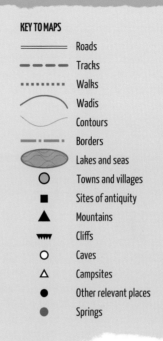

KEY TO MAPS

———	Roads
– – – –	Tracks
··········	Walks
⌒	Wadis
⌣	Contours
·–·–·–·	Borders
⬭	Lakes and seas
○	Towns and villages
■	Sites of antiquity
▲	Mountains
▼▼▼	Cliffs
○	Caves
△	Campsites
●	Other relevant places
●	Springs

Finally, if you are exploring a cave or climbing, you're going to need additional specialist kit.

GPS

We have included GPS Waypoints in route descriptions, initially working with MGRS Position Format and WGS 84 Map Datum, which correlate reasonably well with the 1970s K737 Jordan map series that we have. However, for users of this book, most of whom will not be able to obtain maps other than road maps we have converted the Position Format to degrees, minutes and decimal minutes, which works with Google Earth: simply type the coordinates into the search box without the degree and minute symbols; for example, show N32° 27.654′ E35° 46.593′ as N32 27.654 E35 46.593. We hope the use of GPS points will compensate to some extent for the lack of large-scale maps.

Be prepared!

If you have an accident or get lost it will be up to you to get yourself out, always bearing in mind that there is no official Mountain Rescue Service in Jordan.
As always, what you carry will be a compromise between weight, comfort and safety. However, as mobile phones now work in most parts of Jordan outside the deeper mountain valleys, it is now possible to phone directly for help in emergency. The Royal Jordanian Air Force have carried out a number of helicopter rescues from the mountains of Wadi Rum and Petra, but please don't abuse the system: better to

be self-sufficient if at all possible – even so, it's sensible to include cover for helicopter rescue in your insurance policy.
Useful emergency numbers are:

POLICE **191 / 192**
FIRST AID AND AMBULANCE **193**
PUBLIC SECURITY **196** extn **4661**
(or '**0**') for TOURISM POLICE
CIVIL DEFENCE EMERGENCY **199 / 4617101**
GENERAL EMERGENCY **911**
EMERGENCY (mobile phones only) **112**

Finally and importantly, let someone know not only where you're going, but when you expect to be back and having made this commitment, don't go somewhere else and do check in on your return! Think twice before going caving – there are no specialist mountain, canyon and cave rescue teams in Jordan.

A SPRINGTIME MEADOW WITH FLAX, STAR OF BETHLEHEM AND OTHER FLOWERS

Guides

Many people will be competent enough to walk the treks in this book without a guide, but trekking in Al Ayoun is new and, other than on the Ayoun Trail, people are not yet used to tourists. It can therefore be useful to have a local guide who can be the bridge between you and the locals thereby adding to the cultural aspect of the walk as well as being able to tell you more about the flora and fauna and the history of the area. The guide can also make any accommodation and/or transport arrangements. In 2011, local guides cost from 35-50JD per day dependent on the trek and the size of the group. Other costs will be found in the Appendix.

Grading of walks & treks
Easy walk

Usually no difficulties such as scrambling on rock or scree, no exposure to heights, no steep ascents or descents and no serious route finding problems. Probably less than half a day.

Moderate trek

Altitude differences may be considerable, though usually in a downhill direction! Some easy scrambling may be necessary and experience in route finding is required. Could be one to two days duration.

Serious trek

These routes pass through remote areas, sometimes with unreliable water sources and require a degree of self-sufficiency and experience in wilderness terrain. There could be considerable ascent and descent and route finding experience is essential. Inexperienced parties should take a guide.

PLOUGHING AN AL AYOUN OLIVE GROVE

Rock climbing in Al Ayoun

This book is the first to describe the many cliffs in Al Ayoun, none of which have been equipped with fixed gear, so traditional climbing protection equipment (nuts, cams etc) is needed and the knowledge to use it. See **www.bbc.co.uk/dna/h2g2/alabaster/A390566** for explanations of climbing styles, terminology etc.

For details of cliffs in nearby Ajloun and a glossary of climbing terms see our guide to *Jordan – Walks, Treks, Caves, Climbs & Canyons*. For bigger and more serious climbs see our guide to *Treks & Climbs in Wadi Rum*. Climbers visiting Jordan may like to visit the excellent new indoor climbing wall near Marj al Hammam in the suburbs of Amman, see **www.climbat.com**

Grading of rock climbs

The French system is used, as in Wadi Rum, modern grades going from 1 to 9 in increasing difficulty. Anyone climbing in Jordan will find full details of comparative international rock climbing grading systems in the guide-book to *Treks & Climbs in Wadi Rum*. Stars after the name of the climb indicate the better routes, *** being the best.

Grade 1

The point at which hands are required for balance or safety.

Grade 2

Generally friction slabs or steeper rock with good holds.

Grade 3

The point where the climbing becomes more technical.

Grade 4

Serious climbing requiring climbing competence, special equipment and a knowledge of safety techniques.

Grade 5 and above

These routes are for experienced rock climbers only. Each grade is divided into three categories in increasing order of difficulty, which are, for example, 5a, 5b, 5c, or 5-, 5, 5+.

At the time of writing, the hardest route in this guide is 6a.

TONY HOWARD TOPPING OUT ON THE PILLAR, ARAQ DAMAJ

So far there are few true caves in Jordan and, with the exception of El Hawi pothole, none are technically difficult but Al Ayoun is a karst area and more could be found. Caving is a dangerous business, so take care, as there are no cave rescue teams. Note this advice from a British caving guide: 'When planning a caving trip think of the return journey and remember that caving grades only apply to fit, competent and properly equipped parties; novices in particular will find caves harder than indicated and for most systems there must be sufficient and competent cavers in the party.' Be aware that if you enter an 'active cave', that is, one which still has (or could have) water running through it, it will be subject to flood hazard. If in doubt, don't! Equally important, see 'Caving' for notes on cave conservation.

Grading of caves

Other than the recently discovered pothole of El Hawi, there are no caves in Jordan graded higher than Grade 2 on a commonly used British scale denoting the difficulty and seriousness of caves, which goes from 1 to 5. That does not mean they can be taken lightly – we'll say it again: there are no cave rescue teams in Jordan. Just in case more caves are found, here is a brief résumé of cave grades:

Easy cave

Grade 1 No rope-work or technical difficulties. Route finding may present problems for the uninitiated.

Moderate cave

Grade 2 This includes small potholes. Ropes may be required for ascent and descent. Possibly quite long.

Serious cave

Grade 3 or more Definitely experienced cavers only.

RETURNING FROM THE DEPTHS OF EL HAWI POTHOLE

THE JUDEITA TRAIL, **ROUTE** 12

> Keep close to Nature's heart... and break clear away, once in a while, and climb a mountain or spend a week in the woods. Wash your spirit clean.

John Muir, Early American conservationist, founder of the Sierra Club

THE **ROUTES**

Getting Around

Apart from the Ayoun Trail, the routes are described from south to north, with directions approaching from the villages of Al Ayoun (and for routes further west, from Pella). *See Area Maps* on pages 92–100. See **Contacts** in Appendix for information regarding local transport.

Getting to Al Ayoun

From 7th circle Amman, it's about 43km, 45mins to the intersection near Hadrian's Arch at the southern entrance to Jerash from where there are two options:

1 Via Ajloun

Turn left there to reach Ajloun after another 23km. Continue on, up the long hill to the Ishtafeina junction (traffic lights), turning sharp left for Baoun (the Rasoun road slants down right almost immediately). Continue down the long hill to reach the fourth turning right for Baoun 8km from the top, 79km from Amman. GPS alt. 680m N32° 23.054′ E35° 43.472′. The village centre where four roads meet is a little further on; there's a bakery on the right, also a small café run by Sheikh Hader 100m beyond that on the left and other shops nearby. GPS alt. 660m N32° 23.074′ E35° 43.740′. Total time around 1hr 45mins.

2 The quick way

At the Hadrian's Arch junction, turn left (as above) towards Ajloun and continue up the hill for about 5km turning right (signed Suf) to ascend a steep hill to a pass (Olive Branch Hotel to the right), then down to meet another road. Turn left here and continue through Suf and Ibbin for about 11km to the next T-junction.

Go left again to reach the Ishtafeina junction (traffic lights) in 1.5km. Ajloun is now down to the left. Continue straight on for the approach to Baoun *(see above)* or turn right after 200m to descend directly to Rasoun in about 6km, avoiding left turns for Mihna, Al Yanabia and the RSCN Ajloun Reserve. The RSCN Soap House is on the left, 0.5km beyond Rasoun centre. Orjan is about 2km beyond that, with a café right of the mosque and a bakery in a side street opposite. Baoun is 2km further on round the hillside to the south. Total time 1hr 15mins.

Getting to treks in the area between Al Ayoun & Pella

If starting from Baoun, drive up to the main road just west of the village, turn right and follow it down for 4km to the hairpin bend in the valley bottom:

R2. Wadi Yabis starts at this point following the lane heading downstream to the left. **R7**, ends here, and the Oudeh watermill is 100m upstream to the right (north). This point is 84km from the 7th circle, Amman, 18km from Ajloun, 5km from Baoun.

To reach the next walk, continue on the road, now uphill, for 3km to the big right-hand bend next to Kufr Abil, which is on the left at the top of the hill.

R3. Wadi Salih is the first wadi to be crossed heading north from there on the same road. The walk down starts in the dip 0.5km north of the Kufr Abil junction (pine trees visible down the wadi) and passes the hilltop Greek ruins of Khirbet Sartaba before reaching Pella. The turning for Kufr Awan is almost opposite on the right.

R8. Wadi Sir has two tributaries, the southern one starts about 1.2km further on from the Kufr Awan sign and 0.4km after a small white mosque and minaret on the left of the road; the start of this trek, which visits the Jesus Cave, takes a small track going left (slightly north of west) between houses almost opposite a white house decorated with painted pink diamond motifs on the right side of the road. The Beit Idis traffic lights and the sign to the 'Jesus Cave' are a few hundred metres further on, where the walk down the northern tributary starts. GPS alt. 470m N32° 26.057′ E35° 41.029′.

R9. Wadi abu Salih also offers two routes, the first starts 2km further north again in its southern tributary, just after Kufr Rakib. If approaching from Pella Rest House, go down to the road and turn right then right again in less than 1km and follow the road for about 9km, up past a checkpoint to Kufr Rakib. (Bakery with excellent *taboon* bread just before the crossroads.) Turn left at the crossroads, quickly descending to the point where the road crosses the southern tributary of Wadi abu Salih (usually dry). This is the start of **option 1**, GPS alt. 500m N32° 27.434′ E35° 41.679′. **Option 2** takes the northern tributary, another 1km to the north, starting where the wadi passes beneath the hairpin bend in the main road

just before Ashrafieh, GPS alt. 465m N32° 27.748′ E35° 42.093′. Both walks go to Pella, the northern one being part of **R14**, an enjoyable 2-day trek.

R10. Wadi Taiyiba is about 14km further north along the road, passing Kufr el Ma (the end of **R13**) before going through Deir abu Sa'id (shops and small cafés, 5km from the hairpin bend over Wadi Salih), after which it forks right and soon descends steeply to cross the head of Wadi Ziglab after another 3km. The road to Tibna and the end of **R20** though the Forest of Sirin are in the valley to the right. Continuing along the main road, it then rises immediately uphill, bending east through Sammu before descending to cross Wadi Taiyiba at a big hairpin bend 6km from the Tibna junction.

Getting to treks, caves & cliffs north of Al Ayoun

From Baoun, follow the road that contours along the hillside, heading approx. east out of the village then bending north round a wadi, to reach a roundabout in about 1.8km. Continue straight on to reach a T-junction after another 2.3km. Turn right here (the centre of Orjan with its mosque and café is to the left at GPS alt. 630m N32° 23.750′ E35° 43.955′) and continue, passing signs for Judeita and Wadi Orjan, crossing a small wadi 0.5km after the T-junction. Once over the bridge, turn almost immediately left then follow the road round right and down to the main wadi, 1.3km from Orjan T-junction. GPS alt. 590m N32° 24.206′ E35° 44.247′. Cross the wadi (remains of an old watermill can be seen on the left) before climbing steeply up, turning right past an RSCN supported small-holding selling honey and jam etc. The top of the hill is about 5km from Baoun, and 2km from the wadi, GPS alt. 810m N32° 24.888´ E35° 44.587´. The cliffs of **Araq el Areadh** and **Araq Smeidah** are to the left and right respectively.

The approach for **R12 Judeita Trail** and the **El Hawi pothole** is left here, then immediately right down the hill. Otherwise, turn right here and continue for 2km to where another road comes in from the left from Kufr Rakib and Ashrafieh *(see above)*, GPS alt. 880m N32° 24.933´ E35° 46.065´. At this junction, the cliff of **Al Warda al Hamra** and **R17 The Panoramic Trail** are down to the right.

From this junction, the approach splits to access five treks:

R13. The Zubia Forest Trail is a short way to the north; turn left then immediately right onto a small lane and follow it down for 1km, turning left to finish in a large open area with the Qabla ruins ahead in the trees; a nice location, worth a visit to explore the ruins, and a great place to start a trek from. GPS alt. 830m N32° 25.568´ E35° 45.927´.

R14. The Zubia Forest – Khirbet 'Us 'us – Pella trek starts at the same point as **R13**.

R15. Khirbet 'Us 'us from the Zubia road starts west of the above junction and can be approached by either of the following two routes from Baoun:

Option 1, take the above route to the Qabla junction then turn left as for the

THE ORJAN BAKERY AT THE END OF ROUTE 12, THE JUDEITA TRAIL

Zubia Trail but instead of going down to the right, continue almost 7km towards Ashrafieh, passing the path to **Zubia Cave** after 3km and turning right (north) 2km further on, going downhill to reach trees on the right, just past a cream-coloured house on the same side, and near a pylon (approx. 14km from Baoun). GPS alt. 650m N32° 27.716′ E35° 43.457.

Option 2, follow the road going west from Baoun past Kufr Abil (see above notes on treks to Pella). Immediately on arrival in Ashrafieh, (about 2km **N** of Kufr Abil and 14km from Baoun), just after the big hairpin bend (start of **R9**), turn right and drive up through the village for 3km to 100m before a cream-coloured house on the left. The path to Khirbet 'Us 'us starts here, at a bend in the road where a wall on its left divides a field above from the trees below (GPS point above).

R16. Wadi al Jwanieh as above, follow the approach to **R13** as far as the road junction where that approach turns sharp left, but instead, continue straight on east for approx. 2km along the main road to where a small lane goes down diagonally to the right, this being the start of the walk. GPS alt. 930m N32° 25.275′ E35° 47.303′.

R20. The Forest and Gorge of Sirin follow the approach to **R13** but continue east for a further 1.7km to another road junction, where the road to Rahiba goes sharply left. GPS alt. 1020m N32° 25.452′ E35° 48.235′. Exactly at this point, and directly ahead although out of sight, a lane drops down the hill. Follow it down (it deteriorates badly) to reach a building on the edge of woods after 1.6km (about 12km in total from Baoun). GPS alt. 990m N32° 25.118′ E35° 49.209′.

R5, 12, 13, 14, 15, 16 & 20 may also be approached directly from Amman. Follow the 'quick way' from Jerash (see Getting to Al Ayoun) as far as the T-junction just after Ibbin, but turn right there and drive **NE**, passing 'Afana to reach a road junction in less than 6km. Turn left there for the villages of Rihaba and Zubia, passing a small, rough road, which goes down to the right after 3km, descending to the start of **R20 The Forest & Gorge of Sirin**. At this point, Rihaba is straight ahead and the main road to Zubia and Baoun bends left. Follow this for about 1km to the start of **R16 Wadi al Jwanieh** and just over 1km more to reach the parking place for the cliff of **Al Warda al Hamra** and **R17 The Panoramic Trail**, just before the road junction. For the final approach to **R13 The Zubia Forest Trail**, take the right fork then right again. Take the left fork to continue to Baoun.

R5 starts in the village of Mazar, which is reached via Rihaba (see **R20** above). Just before entering Rihaba, a small lane goes down right at a crossroads, winding almost due north for about 6km, crossing Wadi Sirin, then Wadi esh Sharut just before rising up to reach El Mazar after 6km. **Mazar Cliff** is also reached via Mazar.

R4 starts in Rasoun, as do **R18 The Dolmen Trail** and **R19 The Rasoun – Mar'jam Circuit**.

R6 starts at Mar Elyas, which is signed to the left when arriving in Ishtafeina from the direction of Ajloun (see above). The cliff of **Araq Khalet Hemed** is visible down to the northwest of Mar Elyas.

1-3 Walks & Treks

The true traveller is a guest and thus serves a very real function, even today, in societies where the ideals of hospitality have not yet faded from the 'collective mentality'. To be a host, in such societies, is a meritorious act. Therefore, to be a guest is also to give merit.

Overcoming Tourism, Hakim Bey

Before getting into the 'new' route descriptions, we would like to mention three excellent walks that pass by the Ayoun area and which we have included in the maps in this book (see pages 94–97). To save duplication, we refer you to their descriptions in the 2008 2nd edition of our book to *Jordan – Walks, Treks, Caves, Climbs & Canyons* (see *Appendix* on page 103). They are:

1 Ajloun to Pella

Route 2 in the Jordan guide. A great 2-day trek from Ajloun Castle down to the Greek antiquity site of Pella, finishing down Wadi Salih (**R9** *in the Jordan guide*) and passing though ever-changing scenery. Moderate trek, 36km, 10–12hrs (or 2 days).

A SIMPLE BUT MEMORABLY DELICIOUS AYOUN LUNCH: HOME-GROWN OLIVES, OLIVE OIL WITH GOAT CHEESE, ZATTAR (DRIED WILD THYME) AND FRESH BREAD FROM THE TABOON OVEN

2 Wadi Yabis to the Jordan Valley

Route 5 in the Jordan guide. A thoroughly enjoyable walk down Wadi Yabis starting from the Oudeh watermill in Al Ayoun (see **R7**) and following the wadi down past orchards and olive groves then through a limestone gorge before dropping down to the Jordan Valley. Moderate trek, 12km, 4hrs.

3 Wadi Salih to Pella

Route 9 in the Jordan guide, starting just north of Kufr Abil (see *Getting Around* on page 27). One of our favourite walks down a lovely wadi, initially forested, then pastoral, then climbing to the summit of Khirbet Sartaba with its Greek ruins and great views before descending to Pella. Easy walk, 8km, 3hrs.

There are also other existing walks in the Ayoun area based on the RSCN Woodland Reserve, which is on the hilltop above the village of Orjan. Two of these (**The Prophet's Trail** and **The Orchards Trail**) are described in Routes 3 and 4 in the aforementioned Jordan guide.

The classic introduction to Al Ayoun is **Route 4 The Darb al Ayoun, or Al Ayoun Trail, Rasoun to Mar Elyas.**

See pages 94–97 for area maps.

ROUTE 13, THE ZUBIA FOREST TRAIL

The Darb al Ayoun,
or Al Ayoun Trail, Rasoun to Mar Elyas

One of the best, most enjoyable, most interesting days I have ever spent in Jordan.

*Matthew Teller, author of **The Rough Guide to Jordan***

This popular walk passes through some pleasantly rural and varied scenery, from the irrigated orchards of Wadi Orjan to the wilder scrub and oak forests of the climb to Listib, ending at the ancient hilltop church of Saint Elijah – surely one of the most atmospheric archaeological sites anywhere in Jordan. Listib has been inhabited since at least the Hellenistic era and is believed by some to be the birthplace of the Prophet Elijah; its mosque was built in the Ayyubid period (12th–13thC). On the very summit of the hill, Tel Mar Elyas (Saint Elijah's Hill) was excavated in 1999 and has some of the finest Byzantine mosaics in Jordan, with a Greek inscription of 622AD identifying the site as a church though the location may have long been sacred. There are superb views from the summit.

This walk also passes through the villages of Rasoun, Orjan, and Baoun, and has been designed to allow for the most memorable experience of all: being welcomed into a family home for breakfast, lunch, and an overnight stay. It is also the second day of a new three-day long distance trail, see routes 5 and 6.

The route

From the tourist shelter in Rasoun, GPS alt. 725m N32° 23.928′ E35° 45.652′, follow the road **W** towards Orjan, with opportunities to visit the two RSCN Projects of the Calligraphy House, then the Soap House after about 1km – both worth a visit to learn about calligraphy (and maybe buy a T-shirt to collect later with your name on in Arabic script), and to see how the soap is made using local olive oil and herbs; herbal tea is also available, GPS alt. 750m N32° 24.201′, E35° 45.262′.

From there, take the smaller lane heading down right into the valley with its irrigation channels and remains of water mills, turning left as the lane reaches the perennial stream flowing from springs. Follow the lane along the left side of the wadi for another 1km before turning left, uphill, then right on a smaller track, returning to the wadi. Follow this for another 1km, finally heading steeply up

into the village of Orjan, (bakery, café and shops) GPS alt. 625m N32° 23.792′ E35° 43.981′.

Turn right at the main junction in the village and continue for about 0.5km to

ROUTE 4, AL AYOUN TRAIL, RASOUN TO MAR ELYAS

where the road climbs up left, but instead, keep straight on along a smaller lane, which soon becomes a dirt track with the wadi down below on the right. Follow the track round, descending to reach Wadi abu Karub (Carob tree valley), which is then followed up steeply towards the next village, Baoun. After the track levels out, turn left at a junction, and continue past olive groves and a cemetery to reach Baoun village centre (bakery, café and shops) GPS alt. 665m N32° 23.074′ E35° 43.740′.

With the mosque on your left, turn right then right again and follow the blue arrow directional sign up the one way street for 100m before turning right again at the junction, reaching a second junction in another 150m. Go left here for another 150m then sharply up right on a small steep road heading out of the village. Follow this as it winds around the hillside, now in more open country with good views west across the Jordan Valley to the hills

GRADE
Easy walk, mostly on country lanes.

DETAILS
See map pages 94, 95 and 96. 12km, descending about 150m from 740m before rising to 920m on the summit of Mar Elyas. Local guide essential to benefit from local knowledge along the way and to arrange a lunch or home-stay in the villages of Al Ayoun.

TIME
Allow a full day, 4–5hrs for the walk, plus time in the villages and at Listib and Mar Elyas.

APPROACH
The walk starts in the village of Rasoun, sometimes at the RSCN 'Soap House'.

of Gilboa in Palestine. After about 1km, with the wooded hillside of Mar Elyas immediately ahead to the S, the lane bends right and descends. Leave it here and go left on a shepherd's path heading **SE** between trees into the upper reaches of Wadi Listib. After about 500m the path enters a clearing before crossing below the head of the valley and winding up for 1km to meet a track then a lane going to the ruins of an old mosque at Listib, the small hilltop just **W** of Mar Elyas, GPS alt. 840m N32° 21.961′ E35° 43.100′. The hilltop tell of Mar Elyas is now a short distance to the E, accessible directly or via the road, GPS alt. 910m N32° 21.749′ E35° 43.340′.

Return

You can be met by pre-arranged transport at Mar Elyas (see *Contacts* on page 102) and return to Al Ayoun for home-stay, or continue by **R6**, the next part of the new long distance trail, described on page 36.

THE OLD MOSQUE, LISTIB

Mazar to Rasoun
Day 1

The first day of a three-day trek, though it could be done in two days if you are in a hurry, but why not linger to enjoy the incomparable hospitality of Al Ayoun. The route commences at the hilltop village of El Mazar and passes through deep, forested valleys and alongside orchards and olive groves to the village of Zubia. The route then descends to pass near the seldom-visited Roman ruins of Qabla *(see R13)* before rising to a high viewpoint above one of the area's biggest cliffs, Al Warda al Hamra, from where the end of the walk can be seen far below in Rasoun where a home-stay can be arranged in advance and is well worth the experience.

The route

Walk steeply down the continuation of the lane into, then down, the forested Wadi esh Sharut, which soon meets Wadi Sirin. Follow the lane into Sirin then steeply up the hillside to the right (**S**). Still going uphill, the lane passes a lone farmhouse. (Just above it, a detour can be made along a track, which goes right between fields; at it's end the floor of a vine-press and basin is cut into the limestone.) Back on the road and a little further on, just after a concrete-topped well, turn right onto a grassy lane, GPS alt. 850m N32° 27.249′ E35° 47.128′ about 2km from the start, less than 1hr.

Follow the path to a wall with good views to Wadi Damaj, Wadi Zubia and Ashrafieh (see *R13*), then zig-zag left and down the side of fields on a sometimes-vague path past small olive groves and wheat fields (you may see another ancient vine-pressing floor and basin cut into the limestone). Ahead, a small road is reached. Turn right to a farmhouse, GPS alt. 800m N32° 27.067′ E35° 46.681′. If the owner, Abu Hazim, is there, ask his permission to continue past the house in the same direction, then down the hillside on small paths on rocky ground and through

FORESTED HILLS ON ROUTE 5, MAZAR TO RASOUN

trees (not obvious) to meet a good path. Follow this left round the head of a wadi in nice scenery and continue contouring round until the path becomes a track bending left into the next wadi. Continue steeply up an improving lane to below Zubia at GPS alt. 860m N32° 26.424′ E35° 46.277′, about 2.5km, 1hr from the farmhouse.

Follow roads almost directly up to Zubia, passing right of the large school building then turning left, left again and back right through the village to follow a small road on the S edge of the village heading **SE** above a deep wadi to GPS alt. 910m N32° 25.957′ E35° 46.202′. A steep lane will be seen heading directly down S into the wadi for almost 1km. Go down this and up the continuation path to arrive in a flat field (the car parking area mentioned in **R13**, GPS alt. 830m N32° 25.568′ E35° 45.927′). The Qabla ruins are a short way to the right (**W**). From there, follow the lane S up the hill for 1km to reach the main road with a road junction just to the left at GPS alt. 900m N32° 24.917′ E35° 46.060′.

Cross the road at the junction, and head **SW** down through trees towards the projecting nose of the cliff of **Al Warda al Hamra** visible below, but go right above the nose and contour along the top of the cliff with good views down to Rasoun. Just over 1km from the road, and past the end of the cliff, it becomes possible to descend the rocky, wooded hillside into the valley below Rasoun, keeping right of an olive grove then crossing the valley floor to reach a track, then a road leading up into the village and the end of day one.

GRADE

Moderate walk, always in pleasant scenery with both forests and orchards, sometimes on paths, but frequently along rarely used country lanes. There is quite a lot of ascent and descent, and care is needed with route finding at key points.

DETAILS

See map pages 94, 95 and 99. Approx. 11km, with a total of around 600m of ascent and 680m of descent, some ascents and descents being quite long and steep. Take care to find the connecting paths between roads.

TIME

Allow 5hrs.

APPROACH

See *Getting Around*. From the centre of El Mazar (shops and café) go approx. **W**, close to the upper edge of Wadi esh Sharut for a few hundred metres, then descend steeply into it for a short way to park outside the new Mazar Municipality Centre for Technology and Knowledge. GPS alt. 805m N32° 27.936′ E35° 47.350′.

Day 2 – The Ayoun Trail

See *R4*. 12km from the village of Rasoun to Mar Elyas. If continuing for the final day of the three-day trail, arrange to be met there and taken back to one of the Ayoun villages for a home-stay, returning by car to Mar Elyas in the morning.

Day 3 – From Mar Elyas

The route can then be continued to the Ajloun Castle by *R6*.

6 Tel Mar Elyas to Ajloun Castle
Day 3

This third day has more delightful scenery, passing through deep wadis and thickly wooded hills to emerge beneath one of Jordan's finest Islamic fortresses, Ajloun Castle (Qal'at er Rabad). Built by one of Saladin's generals in 1184, it was an important defence against the Crusaders. Aloof on its hill, it dominates what were the three main routes leading to the Jordan valley and overlooks the hills of Palestine beyond. On a clear day, the cone shaped hill of Mt Tabor, the Biblical 'Hill of Transfiguration' can be seen to the northwest.

The route

Walk down and along the Mar Elyas approach road for about 1km, to the crossroads at GPS alt. 950m N32° 21.293´ E35° 43.821´. Ajloun Castle is visible from there. Cross the road and follow a lane down the left side of the valley for 100m or so, then trend diagonally down into the valley, initially staying above agricultural land, but soon going down into the valley bottom.

Follow this down until the path reaches pylons, turning right up the hillside, onto a small path before reaching the third pylon, GPS alt. 830m N32° 20.708´ E35° 43.846´. (Do not go down to the end of the valley where there is a house with dogs).

WADI NAHLA ON THE WAY TO AJLOUN CASTLE

Instead, follow the path slightly uphill to contour along the right side of the valley before dropping down onto a track just before reaching the main road, about 1.5km, ½hr from the crossroads, GPS alt. 825m N32° 20.526′ E35° 43.736′.

Cross the road directly and walk down a track into the next forested valley, Wadi Nahla. Follow it down keeping to the right side, then moving left before entering the woods, and rising up on a path to below an orchard fence, GPS alt. 780m N32° 20.394′ E35° 43.304′. Descend again into the thickly wooded valley where small intermittent paths continue close to the streambed.

A small cliff showing through the trees on the right side of the valley is passed then a small clearing is reached about 1km from the road (approx. ½hr), GPS alt. 755m N32° 20.355′ E35° 43.043′. A path now slants left up the hillside almost opposite the right end of a wave-shaped cliff on the other side of the valley, which becomes more obvious once you walk up the path a few metres. (A red and white telecom mast can also be seen on the skyline almost directly opposite when walking up this path.) Take care to find this path – it's the key to the way out. Follow it up quite steeply, with some zig-zags and taking care not to lose the trail – it's not always obvious – but generally heading **SSE–SE** up through the trees past GPS alt. 810m N32° 20.283′ E35° 43.043′ and GPS alt. 855m N32° 20.206′ E35° 43.115′. Continue in a similar direction as the trees open out, eventually cresting the hill to meet a wall near a concrete building, GPS alt. 910m N32° 20.109′ E35° 43.248′. The castle can also be

seen across a valley with olive groves.

To avoid agricultural land, go left to the pylon, the next key route marker, and continue right of this to a track, which passes a house and becomes a small road. A little further on, descend right to meet another obvious lane heading across the little valley towards the castle. From the T-junction at the end of the lane, go a short way right on a track below trees then go left keeping close to a wall between woodland and olive groves, cresting the hill to see the castle directly ahead. Descend a lane for 100m then walk up the last little road to reach the castle road exactly at the Visitor Centre, GPS alt. 945m N32° 19.693′ E35° 43.652′.

GRADE
Easy walk, not long, though with quite a lot of ascent, mostly on small paths needing care to find the best way. Guide useful.

DETAILS
See maps on pages 94–95. 7km, descending from 900m at Mar Elyas to 840m then rising along the road to 950m before descending to around 640m in Wadi Nahla, then rising steeply but pleasantly with one small dip across a shallow valley to reach the road below the castle at the Visitor Centre at 945m. The castle is another 50m above at around 1000m. A total of around 380m descent and 480m ascent.

TIME
Allow 3hrs.

APPROACH
The walk starts from the antiquity site of Tel Mar Elyas, GPS alt. 910m N32° 21.749′ E35° 43.340′, where the Ayoun Trail finishes *(see above)*. Mar Elyas is about 10km by road from Ajloun town via Ishtafeina.

7 Wadi Listib to Wadi Yabis

A varied walk, initially with few paths down the wooded Wadi Listib to its junction with Wadi Naum, after which the valley is more open and much easier going. On reaching the confluence with Wadi Yabis the route meets other walks, making a longer trek possible down Wadi Yabis to the Jordan Valley, or even to Pella. *(See routes 2 & 5 in Jordan – Walks, Treks, Caves, Climbs & Canyons, 2008 edition.)*

The route

Follow the dirt track down and round a small hairpin to reach the wadi bed, which soon enters a wooded ravine between the cliffs of **Araq al Hamra** and **Araq Damaj**, passing beyond them after some easy scrambling down the wadi bed. A small but good path is soon found on the left, contouring above the wadi then descending into it where the trees are starting to thin out before rising out on the right side (to Ausara?) just over 1km from the road. GPS alt. 480m N32° 22.633′ E35° 42.474′.

Two telecom masts can be seen on the far horizon at this point. From here, continue once again in the wadi, descending into a rocky section for a short way then emerging into an open area. Beyond, the wadi bends left with a path on its left side, descending into olive groves with a gated fence beyond and another beyond that. If the gates are locked, it's easy to pass the fence. About 1hr from the start of the wadi. The improving path now rises very obviously up the right bank below another fence then meets a small road winding down from Ausara (above on the right). 3.5km from the start of the trek, less than 2hrs. GPS alt. 390m N32° 22.571′ E35° 41.319′.

Cross the lane to reach another olive grove and follow a track above on the right,

SPRINGTIME IN WADI NAUM, ROUTE 7, WADI LISTIB TO WADI YABIS

avoiding crops to soon reach another lane (also going to Ausara?). **R1** from Ajloun to Pella – see above – enters the valley from the S at this point, coming down Wadi Naum on its second day.

Leave the lane for the good track on the right of the valley above ancient olive groves with huge trees. Further down some strange, smooth sided, bulbous boulders will be seen, some egg shaped, some round, some with whorls; they are probably 'limestone concretions', formed by sediment built up in successive layers round a shell or stone. You can contemplate their geological origin as you continue along the track until it bends up sharply right opposite a side valley on the left.

Here, descend to Wadi Naum to join the Ajloun–Pella trek. About 5km, 2½hrs from the start of Wadi Listib. Continue on paths or in the wadi bed (usually dry) passing through a small ravine of limestone-based conglomerate before emerging into flat open meadows. Continue on improving paths to reach a final olive grove.

There are some beehives on the right and a concrete irrigation channel bridges the streambed. Just beyond, the track reaches the old mill at the junction with Wadi Yabis, (*R5 in the Jordan guide*) where there is a permanent encampment with dogs that may be off their chains with no-one looking after them – have your trekking pole ready, or let them see you picking up some stones, though hopefully there will be no need to throw them!

This point is just over 3hrs from the start. The Ajloun–Pella trek crosses the stream here and climbs up to Kufr Abil before descending to Pella via the delightful Wadi Salih (**R3**), whilst the

GRADE
Easy walk with some easy scrambling down Wadi Listib.

DETAILS
See maps on pages 95–96. About 1km from the end of the lane **SW** of Baoun (almost 1.5km from Baoun centre) from where the route rises from 640m to 690m at the head of the wadi before descending to 220m at the Yabis junction.

TIME
3hrs if starting from the head of the wadi to the finish at Oudeh watermill; add an extra ½hr if walking from Baoun.

APPROACH
From Baoun village, either walk or drive the first 1.5km following lanes on the Ayoun Trail *(see above)* to the point where the lane finally bends right and descends, with the wooded hillside of Mar Elyas immediately ahead to the S. Close by, a dirt track descends diagonally right down the side of Wadi Listib.
GPS alt. 690m N32° 22.513′ E35° 43.425′.

Yabis trek (**R2**) continues down the valley for a further 3½hrs. Our route goes up the road on the right for 1km alongside pomegranate trees to meet the main Kufr Abil–Baoun road at a hairpin bend near the Oudeh watermill, a short way upstream.

Return
Either pre-arrange transport back to Al Ayoun (see *Contacts* on page 102) or hitch a ride back up the road (you may be asked to pay, although it's only 4km so not expensive).

Alternative return
Continue to the Jordan Valley down Wadi Yabis (**R2**) or via The Ajloun–Pella trek and Wadi Salih (**R1** and **R3**).

Wadi Sir & the Jesus Cave

The first part of this walk includes the Jesus Cave antiquity site and a ruined Byzantine Church, which some may find sufficient in itself. However, the full trek, as described here, then continues all the way down Wadi Sir to Pella providing a good day's walk with varied scenery. As always in north Jordan, it's at its best in the spring. Alternatively the wadi can be followed in its entirety without diverting to the cave and church. This is of less interest and the stony nature of the upper wadi detracts a little from what is otherwise a very enjoyable route.

The route

Option 1

From the last house a path can be seen descending left towards a bend in the wadi. The minaret of the mosque near the Jesus Cave can also be seen in that direction (**NW**) on top of the opposite side of the wadi. That is the first objective.

Follow the path easily down to reach the valley at GPS alt. 420m N32° 26.162′ E35° 41.092′. Now follow the wadi down a short way to the next bend where a good path rises out diagonally to the right. As it nears the top of the hill, it bends left and goes directly towards the mosque. Once there, take a track just left of the mosque then go right to find the Jesus Cave, ½hr. The local name for the cave is *Kahf el Messih* (Cave of the Messiah) in the belief that Jesus stayed here before being baptised in the Jordan River by John the Baptist. There are Roman period burial alcoves cut in the rock, whilst outside there are millstones and an area for treading grapes, with channels and basins to collect the juice. A gnarled oak, the roots of which descend into a cistern carved into the rock, provides shade and is venerated by locals. GPS alt. 500m N32° 26.504′ E35° 40.882′.

Now, continue down a small lane and turn left after about 300m to find an old house with a huge cavern (water cistern?) below – origin and purpose unknown to the authors, GPS alt. 480m N32° 26.414′ E35° 40.696′. Return to the small lane and follow it a short way to its end then continue down a little more with agricultural land on the right before heading right up the hillside to reach walls. Keep them on your left before crossing the outer one to reach a dead tree from where a grassy lane leads pleasantly between fields directly to a lane across which are the ruins of a Byzantine church and tombs. 1km from the mosque, ½hr max, 1hr from the start, GPS alt. 475m N32° 26.756′ E35° 40.339′.

From the church go **W** along the lane, which stops near the edge of a small valley leading down left. Follow this valley down into Wadi Sir and so to Pella. (Looking down from the top we saw a good path on the right of, and about 50m above, the wadi bed. This looks better than walking in the stony streambed as we did originally – see below). Alternatively, avoid this descent and continue W out onto the headland, which has more ruins, then descend quite steeply to reach the wadi (seen by the authors but not checked).

Option 2

For anyone wanting to follow the wadi throughout, the trek can be started from the road signed to the 'Jesus Cave' just after the Beit Idis traffic lights (see *Getting around* on page 27), GPS alt. 530m N32° 26.525′ E35° 41.560′.

From the road, follow the wadi down W, most of this initial section being in the stony wadi bed or on stony ground as there are few paths. Nevertheless, the meandering narrow valley itself is, as always in this area, very pretty in spring. After 1.5km a path is reached entering from the left, from the road above – this is the entrance taken by Option 1. Another 1km further on the wadi then enters a little gorge with rough going, eventually passing below the Byzantine Church, 2hrs, 5km from the start. Option 1 re-enters the valley here for the final 6km, GPS alt. 350m N32° 26.811′ E35° 39.818′.

GRADE

Easy walk (some route finding necessary for the diversion to the cave and church and back into the wadi).

DETAILS

See maps on pages 95 and 97. 10km all the way to Pella (only 2km if finishing at the ruined church). The route descends through various eco-systems from 500m to sea level at the Pella Rest House, but rises 60m along the way to reach the Jesus Cave then descends and rises 40m to reach the church ruins. A final short ascent to the Pella Rest House makes a total of 500m of descent and 150m of ascent).

TIME

An easy hour to the ruined church. 4–5hrs all the way to Pella.

APPROACH

See *Getting around*.

TOMBS AND OLIVE PRESS NEAR THE JESUS CAVE

To continue down Wadi Sir (Options 1 & 2)

Follow the streambed down (look for a path above on the right), until just over 1km further on the valley begins to open out and another wadi enters from the right. After another 1km the Pella–Kufr Rakib road can be seen just above, and after further 1km a small lane is reached crossing the wadi. Just beyond, the streambed goes over cliffs, dropping into the ravine of Wadi el Jirm, which leads to Pella.

There is a track opposite, alongside the wadi, but don't enter the valley directly. Instead go right, up the road for 100m or so, then take the obvious dirt track left onto the pine covered, steep hillside high above the gorge. Follow this down for about 1km until the track can be seen descending into the wadi bed. At that point another smaller path contours out right, along the hillside, to reach the fence of the Pella antiquity site after 0.5km. Follow the fence up the hillside and round to the left to reach a path going directly up to the Rest House and a welcome drink. GPS alt. zero m N32° 27.027′ E35° 37.062′.

Return

Either pre-arrange accommodation in the Countryside Hotel at Pella with the Rest House Manager (see *Contacts* on page 101), or ask if he can arrange for a taxi back up to Al Ayoun.

FLOWERS FILL THE LOWER SLOPES OF WADI SIR ABOVE PELLA

APPROACHING THE BYZANTINE CHURCH RUINS

Wadi abu Salih to Pella

There are two optional starts and finishes to the route: Option 1, which follows the wadi all the way to the hot springs is more challenging, but Option 2, which is also part of R14 (a contrasting one or two-day walk to Pella) is nicer walking and has good views across the Jordan Valley to Palestine.

The route

Option 1

Follow the southern tributary of the wadi down through olive groves and fields (keep to the edges to avoid trampling crops) and pass a small path, which crosses the valley. Continue down on vague and intermittent paths until a valley enters from the right, this being the route taken by the start of Option 2.

Continue down the valley past occasional sturdy Mediterranean oaks, and with pines high above on the right, until it narrows and a little scrambling is necessary before it opens out again and meets another track crossing the valley. A little further on, another small lane enters the valley about 5km from the start. Follow this down a short way, descending right into the wadi when the track starts to rise away from it (see *Option 2*). The streambed (dry in April 2008) now enters a narrow ravine where scrambling is necessary (beware flash floods). At its end there may be a murky pool, GPS alt. 165m N32° 28.120′ E35° 38.952′.

Continue through more narrows with steep sides of soft white rock and caves high on the right, changing sides as and when necessary; towards the end some scrambling in the oleander-choked stream bed may be necessary before emerging onto more open but still steep terrain on the right bank, leading to a dirt track, GPS alt. 160m N32° 28.356′ E35° 38.271′

where ruined dolmens are located. Follow the track down for almost 2km to the rock arch and hot spring (busy on Fridays). GPS alt. minus 60m N32° 27.915′ E35° 37.209′. Either descend to the spring or cross the natural arch before walking 2km generally **S** on the road (avoid the big hairpin bend by going up a steep path on the scree covered hillside); continue **S** to reach the turn up left to the Rest House.

Option 2

Part of **R14**. It's possible to walk directly down the wadi from the hairpin bend below and **S** of Ashrafieh (previously named Khanzira), about 1.5km **N** of Kufr Rakib), GPS alt. 470m N32° 27.749′ E35° 42.099′, but the best way is to go up the road towards Ashrafieh for 5mins, to reach a small store on the right (soft drinks, canned food, biscuits etc) then a mosque on the left. GPS alt. 490m N32° 27.787′ E35° 41.889′.

Turn left here to follow a small lane, which soon becomes a dirt track descending to reach the wadi in a further 5mins. The path soon crosses to the left side of the valley, moving back to the right before reaching some pines (also on the right). Continue in the wadi bed to meet the southern tributary from Kufr Rakib (see *Option 1 above*) 2km from the start (¾hr).

Now continue down the wadi, crossing a small lane to meet a dirt track that leads easily and enjoyably up and out onto the ridge left (**S**) of the valley and high above Pella (possible campsite above the track, but no water). There are superb views out to the volcanic cone of Mt Tabor and the Gilboa Hills in Palestine near Nazareth, the start of the ten-day Nativity Trail to Bethlehem. In the night, the lights of the illegal Israeli settlements can be seen on the West Bank hilltops. The track now descends, still with great views, eventually reaching a small road, which is followed down to just above the road that runs from the Hot Springs to Pella. An obvious short cut leads down scree to that road, meeting Option 1 again at GPS alt. minus 20m N32° 27.641′ E35° 37.361′. From there it's just over 1km to the Pella Rest House (see *Option 1*).

Return

Either pre-arrange accommodation in the Countryside Hotel at Pella with the Rest House Manager (see *Contacts* on page 101), or ask if he can arrange for a taxi back up to Al Ayoun.

GRADE
OPTION 1, Moderate trek; OPTION 2, easy walk.

DETAILS
See maps on pages 95, 96, 97 and 99.

OPTION 1 – THE VALLEY ROUTE. 12km, with walking and scrambling on steep terrain and sometimes tricky route finding. The route starts in the southern tributary of the wadi and descends from 500m to 60m below sea level at the natural arch and hot springs, then ascends the road to Pella Rest House at sea level.

OPTION 2 – THE HILL ROUTE. 11km, pleasant easy walking, almost always on paths or tracks. The route starts in the northern tributary and descends from 500m to 180m then follows a track rising gently over a hill south of the wadi, reaching 230m before descending to meet the road to the Pella Rest House at 20m below sea level and finishing at the Rest House, a total of 100m of ascent and 600m descent.

TIME
Allow 4–5hrs for OPTION 1, (4hrs to the hot spring and another ½hr to the Rest House) and 4hrs for OPTION 2.

APPROACH
See *Getting around*.

GOOD LOCAL FOOD IN THE BAOUN CAFÉ

TORTOISES ARE OFTEN SEEN IN SPRINGTIME

Wadi Taiyiba to the Jordan Valley

Long and varied, descending 600m through different ecosystems and geological layers and past olive groves, orchards, an abandoned fish farm and a ruined water-powered flour mill to almost 200m below sea level. There is even rumoured to be an underground church.

The route

From GPS alt. 390m N32° 31.236′ E35° 44.875′ follow the wadi bed down as it twists and turns between cliffs with numerous cave-like holes, passing an olive grove after 3km, 1hr. 1km further on, a path enters down a wooded valley on the left, GPS alt. 260m N32° 31.548′ E35°43.501′. After another 3km, past hillsides of oaks and pines, with a variety of birds and the occasional olive grove, a small lane enters steeply from the left, from Jinnin es Safa, 2km to the S, crosses the wadi and becomes a washed-out track rising N for 2km to Taiyiba, (approx. 6km from the start, 2hrs – having started late, we spent the night here).

The valley now opens out for a while, with small wheat fields (April) but paths continue along their edges, eventually crossing the wadi to join a track coming down W from Taiyiba GPS alt. 160m

N32° 32.265′ E35°40.071′, about 3hrs, 10km from the start. Follow the track along the right bank of the wadi to opposite a Bedouin-type camp with abandoned fish ponds just beyond, at which point the track starts to rise away from the wadi bed, which is filled with fragmites reeds and oleanders and a small stream (April). Leave the track and walk down alongside the wadi for 1km to the ruins of a flourmill (*tahouneh*). The channel that fed water to the mill is now dry, but cut stones can be seen where a sluice gate used to allow excess water out of the channel back into the wadi. The channel itself leads to the first of two consecutive shafts that drop vertically through two tiers of the old mill, to drive the millstones. (Whilst we were there, a farmer arrived with his donkey from the camp upstream to fill water bottles at

A CHAMELEON

the adjacent pool in the wadi, and told us that there is "A place of worship, or church, in a cave a little further down the valley". It may well be true, but we didn't find it.)

From there, small paths can be seen along either side of the wadi, but we took the old man's advice and followed a larger track rising up easily right to orchards, olive groves and a ruined house of traditional architecture where stone arches compensate for the lack of timber for roof beams. The track continues up past the house with citrus and pomegranate trees on the left, their red flowers in bloom (April), and giant prickly pear cactus with their yellow flowers bordering the right of the path. Where the track begins to climb the hill more directly, we continued **W** through the upper olive grove, losing the path but emerging onto the hillside to see another track descending from above, just across a small wadi, GPS alt. 10m N32° 32.269´ E35° 38.744´. It's probably best to avoid the olive grove by going above it and crossing the hillside to meet the track.

Either way, once on the track, follow it down steeply until it splits, one path descending an isthmus of land between two streambeds into the wadi, the other contouring the steep hillside high above the wadi. We took the top track but the easier looking bottom track follows the oleander-filled wadi down a short way then climbs back out to meet the upper track, so both options are possible.

Continue across the steep, white hillside until the path descends into the wadi, now choked with vegetation. Again, two options are possible: a 3m climb up loose but easy white rock on the right leads to a track which contours **W** across the steep

GRADE
Easy walk but long, though with reasonably straight-forward route finding.

DETAILS
See map on page 98. Though sometimes small, there are paths the whole way down the valley, following the wadi for 20km from the upper plateau at 400m to the Jordan valley road in the village of Waqqas at 190m below sea level. There may be murky pools just after half way, past the old flourmill, but as always, it's best to carry sufficient water.

TIME
Allow 6–7 hours.

APPROACH
About ½hr by taxi (10JD in 2008) from Pella Rest House, a little more from Baoun (see *Getting around*). The route starts just before the bottom of the long hairpin just over 1km after Sammu, entering the wadi where it winds **W** through a twisting limestone gorge with old quarry workings below.

hillside or, follow the track through the oleanders until both tracks meet. Continue along this good track eventually passing a hot spring emerging from a pipe. Just beyond, a surfaced road is reached with numerous Bedouin camps above. 2km further on past the village school, the Jordan Valley road is reached in Waqqas (bread shop and groceries), GPS alt. minus 190m N32° 32.219´ E35° 36.103´.

Return
It's about 10km S to Tabqat Fahl and the Pella Rest House by frequent bus and/or local taxi (5JD for taxi in 2008), or arrange transport and accommodation with the Rest House Manager (see *Contacts* on page 101).

RSCN Campsite to Baoun
via Wadi el 'Alaqa

An easy and enjoyable short walk down through woods and past olive groves and orchards to the village of Baoun, where it finishes in the square near the mosque and the café. The first kilometre of the route is the same as the Prophet's Trail from RSCN to Mar Elias (**R3** in the Jordan guide).

The route

Walk down through trees to reach a lane, which is followed to the right for a short way to a pylon on the left, GPS alt. 985m, N32° 22.529′ E35° 45.701′. (It may continue up to the RSCN gates.) A small path goes down left under the pylon to enter an orchard in the valley bottom, then going right into the tree-filled Wadi Shiteau. Follow the (usually dry) streambed down though the dense woodland of Mediterranean oak and past occasional smooth red-barked strawberry trees, usually on small but reasonable paths but sometimes steep and rocky in or alongside the stream, until the trees thin out and the stream joins Wadi Al 'Alaqa. A little over 1km from the start (¾hr). GPS alt. 820m N32° 22.572′ E35° 45.204′.

Ahead are olive groves. Keep high on the right to avoid them, soon meeting a dirt road that follows the side of the valley down through nice scenery to where Wadi es Sus joins it on the left, from the **S** after another 1km, 20mins. GPS alt. 720m,

MAKING BREAD WITH HERBS IN A TABOON OVEN, AL AYOUN

N32° 22.520′ E35° 45.698′. A small but surfaced road continues down the valley from here reaching houses on the outskirts of Baoun after about 1km. Continue along this road pleasantly enough for another 1km into and through the upper part of Baoun, passing a school before reaching the village square with its bakery after a further half hour from Wadi es Sus. Take the first road back to the right for about 50m to find Sheikh Hader's café on the left with shops opposite.

Return

If you are staying at the RSCN Campsite, pre-arrange a lift with RSCN, otherwise arrange a taxi up from Baoun.

GRADE
Easy walk. Sometimes a bit steep and rocky in the initial wadi.

DETAILS
See map on page 95. 4km. Downhill almost all the way, descending 370m, from 1020m to 650m.

TIME
Less than 2hrs.

APPROACH
The walk starts a few hundred metres outside the RSCN Campsite, leaving the approach road just after a house on the right when coming from RSCN, at GPS alt. 1020m, N32° 22.614′ E35° 45.782′. (A direct approach from the RSCN gates may be possible but we didn't get chance to check.)

AL AYOUN HOSPITALITY, FRESH FROM THE GARDENS, ORCHARDS AND HILLS

THE AUTHORS ENJOY A SMALL LUNCH!

12 The Judeita Trail

A varied and enjoyable trek despite lots of descent and ascent. Though much of it is on country lanes, they are almost all quiet and seldom if ever frequented except by local farmers tending their orchards and olive groves. The route initially descends through a rural idyll in a secluded wooded valley, once home to a saintly man and a place where local people used to pray. It then rises gently up to the outskirts of Judeita with panoramic views over Al Ayoun, only to plunge down a helter-skelter steep and winding lane to the depths of Wadi Orjan before rising again to the village of Orjan with its welcome café.

The route

Walk down the track, which soon becomes a grass track descending very pleasantly first though olive groves, then through the forest, to emerge at more olive groves in the bottom of Wadi el Hawi, at which point it meets an old lane. Follow this **SW** along the quiet rural valley past orchards and olive groves passing a road junction after half an hour, where the Judeita lane begins to climb up hill to the left, GPS alt. 565m N32° 25.052′ E35° 42.964′. It's possible to continue down the valley to meet the road

going to the hairpin bend at the Oudeh Watermill and the start of Wadi Yabis (**R2**), but our preferred finish takes you up the hill to Judeita or, better still, Orjan.

Follow the lane easily up for about 10mins, pleasantly gaining height to about 100m or so before the top, where a track goes up left, GPS alt. 595m N32° 24.989′ E35° 42.752′ to cross over a ridge and descend left along the side of a small valley. Once near the valley bottom go down right, onto an obvious

DESCENDING WADI EL HAWI

path that crosses the valley and climbs up past tall Cypress trees. Ignore the first path branching left alongside a wall, and continue a little further to the next small but obvious path, GPS alt. 610m N32° 24.686′ E35° 42.753′. At this point there are two options, those finishing in Judeita should continue along the main path for about 0.5km into the village to meet pre-arranged transport. To continue the walk to Orjan, follow the small path left, slanting up the right edge of olive groves to meet a small road below the mosque. Follow this up and right to the main road and go left to a second mosque, passing a small shop selling drinks etc, then cross the road and head for two telecom masts, GPS alt. 670m N32° 24.452′ E35° 42.926′.

Go left, beneath the masts, and follow the lane around the hillside, passing between houses and soon passing a crossroads with another small shop on

GRADE

Easy walk, a 'family trail' on country lanes as far as Judeita where you can pre-arrange to be met for a lift back to Al Ayoun. Moderate Trek if you continue all the way to Orjan.

DETAILS

See maps on pages 95 and 96. 6km to Judeita with around 100m of descent and ascent. 9km for the full walk, descending about 400m in total from 770m and rising a total of 300m to 660m at Orjan, the last 0.5km of ascent to the village being the steepest.

TIME

Allow 2½hrs for the walk to Judeita, 3½hrs for the walk to Orjan.

APPROACH

A vehicle is needed to drive up the road to the top of the hill above Orjan as for **R13** (see *Getting Around*). Turn left there, then immediately right and continue about 2km down a narrow, rough lane to the first junction on the left, GPS alt. 770m N32° 25.890′ E35° 44.278′.

APPROACHING ORJAN

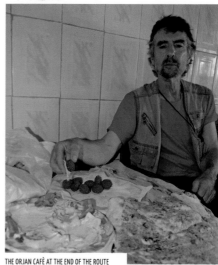

THE ORJAN CAFÈ AT THE END OF THE ROUTE

the left (drinks etc) before continuing with great views soon opening out over Al Ayoun and down to Wadi Yabis in the **W**, to reach a T-junction about 10mins from the masts. Turn left and continue down to another T-junction, turning right and descending a crazily steep and loosely gravelled road past olive groves. The lane soon turns into a grass track from where the stream can be heard down below in the lush valley of Orjan. The angle eases as it continues down to stepping-stones across the fast-flowing wadi, GPS alt. 515m N32° 23.877′ E35° 43.654′.

Once across the stream follow the path up steeply past fig and pomegranate orchards, then ancient olive groves (some trees are 6m in girth!). The path emerges in Orjan on a small lane. Go left and right to pass a bakery (excellent bread, which we tried to buy, but the baker wouldn't take any money even though we were total strangers). The village square is just ahead, with its mosque and shops, and a café selling hummus, falafels, full, tea and soft drinks. Enjoy!

WADI ORJAN

APPROACHING JUDEITA

13 The Zubia Forest Trail
or Qabla Trail

A unique and very enjoyable walk in a beautifully forested valley starting from the ruins of Qabla (possibly Roman) from where there are good views down the wadi, but no signs of a path and you really wonder if the trek will be possible. It is however a wonderful day out following a good path all the way down the valley then up to the village of Kufr el Ma above the Jordan Valley. Along the way, an optional side trail leads up to the location of Khirbet 'Us 'us, offering an opportunity to extend the trek all the way to Pella, perhaps camping on the way (*R14*).

The route

Leave Qabla at two big rock-hewn cisterns, Birqat Qabla, to the left of an area of flat limestone, just after the actual ruins. GPS alt. 840m N32° 25.541′ E35° 45.827′. The valley floor is just below to the left and a small path will be found entering the forest. Follow it down meeting another path coming in from the right down Wadi Wa'ra alongside a streambed (probably dry). Continue, sometimes crossing the dry wadi, sometimes in it (beware of flash floods!). In less than ½hr another wadi enters from the right. Continue down, always following the stream and rarely more then 10m from it, ignoring any side paths that may head off up the hillsides.

The walk is mostly in forest with the occasional clearings filled with flowers in the spring. There are also frequent signs of woodcutting (probably illegal). Less than 1hr from the start the path goes through an especially picturesque clearing where the stream passes through rock basins holding pools of water after rain. GPS alt. 670m N32° 26.268′ E35° 44.961′.

A little further on, a track enters from the right (from Zubia village?). This soon leads to signs of digging and two adjacent cave entrances known as Ain Zubia (Zubia Spring) as both caves contain water (see *Caving*). About 3km, 1hr, from the start of the trek. GPS alt. 630m

THE ZUBIA FOREST TRAIL

N32° 26.704′ E35° 44.652′. Continue down the valley, still on paths, passing by an old olive grove on the left where a wide valley, Wadi Damaj, enters from the right after another 3km, GPS alt. 550m N32° 27.459′ E35° 44.075′ (6km in total, around 2hrs).

The site of Khirbet 'Us 'us is hidden in trees above on the left, but is accessible up a track (see *R14* and *R15*). Further on, the village of Tibna can be seen ahead high on the right side, then two long narrow olive groves on the left side of the wadi are passed. 5mins further on, a path leaves the wadi, and rises diagonally up the left side. This is the way to Kufr el Ma, about 9km, 3-3½hrs, from the start. GPS alt. 440m N32° 28.776′ E35° 43.202′. (If you miss the exit path, you will soon reach an olive grove on the right side of the wadi – go back!)

Follow the path up, passing beneath then above cliffs and finally through pines before reaching a wide dirt track. Follow this in the same **WNW** direction, still rising

GRADE
Easy walk.

DETAILS
See maps on pages 95, 96 and 99. 13km, descending from 840m at Qabla to 440m before leaving the wadi and rising over the shoulder of a hill to 490m then descending to the main road in Kufr el Ma at 340m, a total of 50m ascent and 550m descent. Route finding is reasonably straightforward but take care in locating the exit from the valley.

TIME
4–5hrs.

APPROACH
Driving from Baoun, it's less than ½hr to the start (see *Getting around*).

up to meet a road. This reaches Kufr el Ma in about 0.5km then descends through the town to reach the main road opposite a mosque with a tall slender turquoise minaret of perforated metal. There are shops to the left selling drinks etc, and a bakery with good *taboon* bread, GPS alt. 360m N32° 28.976′ E35° 41.388′.

Return
The easiest return is to take a taxi 16km back to Baoun (numerous minibuses pass along the main road looking for business). Or it may be possible to hitch a ride, or pre-arrange transport in Al Ayoun to drop you off at the start and collect you at the end (see *Contacts* on page 102).

The start of the above route can be combined with **R9** to give **R14** The Zubia Forest – Khirbet 'Us 'us – Pella trek.

VIEW UP ROUTE 13 THE ZUBIA FOREST TRAIL, FROM KHIRBET 'US 'US

14 The Zubia Forest – Khirbet 'Us 'us – Pella trek

A wonderful combination of walks, full of variety and interest as it passes through various ecosystems from Roman ruins in forested Mediterranean hill country to Greco-Roman Pella above the sub-tropical Jordan valley.

The route

Descend Wadi Zubia (**R13**) then after the olive grove on the left (about 6km, 2hrs, see **R13**), take the track up left. This goes almost due **W** to reach a clearing on the shoulder of the hill after about 2–300m, location of Khirbet 'Us 'us. Directly ahead in a limestone hollow is a *bir* or cistern cut into the rock. GPS alt. 590m N32° 27.435′ E35° 43.933.′

There are olive groves just ahead in a small valley and also to the right where a farmer from the village of Tibna was working. He told us that the nearby *bir* was of Roman origin and showed us other incut basins containing water. He also pointed out the location of a number of caves, some with carved niches, just up the hillside with beautiful views across Zubia forest (reached by a small diversion uphill and diagonally left). Whether or not they had been tombs as the farmer believed was not clear, but they had obviously been used as shelters as evidenced by the smoke covered roofs. GPS alt. 620m N32° 27.344′ E35° 43.869′.

Back at the *bir*, the continuation path up though the forest beyond is almost directly opposite, across an olive grove in a small valley. It is not easily seen but an electricity pylon visible on the skyline is

CAMP HIGH ABOVE THE JORDAN VALLEY

a useful landmark. Nearby identification points are a large white limestone boulder 20m left of the point where the path enters the forest, and a less obvious old supporting wall at its start. Take care to find the path as otherwise you will have to struggle up through the jungle!

First, descend to the olive grove, skirting round to the left then back right on the other side to find the white rock and the little retaining wall beyond. The path then winds up enjoyably through the trees, generally **NW** and eventually meeting a low wall. Keep this on your right until it ends and another one starts on the left. Follow the right side of this up to the road. 1km, 20mins, arriving about 100m below a cream coloured house on the left of the road GPS alt. 650m N32° 27.716′ E35° 43.457′.

Now follow the road down pleasantly towards Ashrafieh (previously known as Khanzira) for about 10mins before turning diagonally left into ancient olive groves, quickly meeting a path going across the valley, then leaving it after a short way to continue the diagonal route across to the left (**S**) side of the valley to meet another lane. Follow this down, almost to the valley bottom. At that point another track climbs steeply up left, then a dirt track goes right into the top of some olive groves. Go though the groves (take care with walls) to reach a wild hillside of pines and limestone rocks, which leads enjoyably down right, but trending left to reach the valley floor just 200m from the hairpin bend immediately S of Ashrafieh and about 2.5km from the road above 'Us 'us. 11km, 4hrs from Qabla, junction with the start of **R9**. GPS alt. 460m N32° 27.752′ E35° 42.102′.

GRADE
Moderate trek.

DETAILS
See maps on pages 95, 96, 97 and 99. 22km, descending from 840m at Qabla to sea level at Pella with about 100m of ascent from Wadi Zubia to the hilltop road above Khirbet 'Us 'us then another 60m or so between there and Ashrafieh, then 600m of descent and 100m of ascent between there and the Pella Rest House where a short ascent is soon rewarded by a refreshing drink! About 1100m of descent in total and 260m of ascent. Route finding is reasonably straightforward but needs particular care for the section from Wadi Zubia to Ashrafieh. There are shops in Ashrafieh where basic food and drinks can be bought. If required, pre-arrange accommodation in Pella (see *Contacts* on page 101).

TIME
About 9hrs, but nice to split into two easy days, camping (or bivouacking) above Khirbet 'Us 'us near the cave shelters (about 6km from the start), or above Pella on the last hilltop (about 18km from the start); great views from either, especially above Pella. There is no water at either site unless you are lucky and there is some in the cistern at 'Us 'us. You could stock up at Ashrafieh if camping above Pella.

APPROACH
As for **R13**.

The northern tributary of Wadi abu Salih starts below the bend, but as recommended in **R9** Option 2, go up the road a short way to Ashrafieh and the shops before continuing to Pella by that route (11km).

Return
Pre-arrange transport inAl Ayoun or with Dib Hussein at Pella where there is also accommodation (see *Contacts* on page 102).

Khirbet 'Us 'us from the Zubia Road

A pleasant short descent to a nice area in the beautiful forested valley of Zubia with options to explore 'Roman caves', continue to the Roman ruins of Qabla or the village of Kufr el Ma, or just return.

GRADE
Easy walk but take care with route finding.

DETAILS
See maps on pages 95, 96 and 99. Less than 1km each way with an altitude difference of only 60m, but can be extended another 6km either by following Wadi Zubia **E** to Qabla, rising about 270m (the reverse of the start of **R13**), or **W** to Kufr el Ma (the latter half of **R13**), descending a total of 250m with a climb of 50m out of the wadi at half way.

TIME
Allow 2hrs to visit and explore the area around Khirbet 'Us 'us and return to the start; add an extra 2hrs for the ongoing options.

APPROACH
See *Getting Around*.

The route
Follow the path along the upper edge of the trees keeping left of the wall until it ends and another wall starts below. Follow the right side of this down into the forest where the path then winds down to emerge on the edge of an olive grove in a little valley. The *bir* or 'Roman well' is directly opposite, but detour round to the right to reach it. There are some cave shelters and good views of the valley a short way up to the right. Remember where the path emerges from the trees as you will need to find it if you are returning that way (see *Details and GPS points* in *R13*).

If you are continuing up or down Zubia Valley, the continuation track to Wadi Zubia is directly ahead beyond the *bir* and reaches the wadi in 200m or so. From there follow **R13** up or down the valley.

Return
Wherever you finish you will need to have pre-arranged a taxi (see *Contacts* on page 102), or it might be possible to hitch, though not from Qabla from where you would have to walk another 1km to reach the road.

CHATTING WITH AN OLIVE FARMER, KHIRBET 'US 'US

THE WAY UP FROM KHIRBET 'US 'US IS ALMOST HIDDEN IN THE FOREST

Not easy walking – it is frequently necessary to squeeze between or under trees and the wadi bed, which is often the only way to go, is rough and stony.

GRADE

See map on page 95. Moderate trek, short, but some scrambling including a 10m down-climb, grade 2.

DETAILS

5km. In or close to the wadi most of the way, so not recommended if flooding is possible. Descends 280m from 960m to 680m before rising steeply for 50m to finish in Rasoun.

TIME

2½hrs.

APPROACH

See *Getting Around*.

A TRICKY DESCENT ON ROUTE 16

The route

Walk down the lane a short way before cutting right down the hillside fields to reach the wadi bed (hopefully dry). Follow it down into the woods and continue in or alongside the wadi (occasional paths) to reach the junction with Wadi Saqqaya (which provides an alternative start from the S). Approx. 1km from the start.

After about 1.5hrs always following or in the streambed (some scrambling) the E end of the impressive cliff of **Al Warda al Hamra** (see *Climbing* on page 84) can be seen above to the right. A little further on, the wadi narrows to a small gorge, dropping down limestone slabs then over a 10m drop. Descend this with care (grade 2) moving left or right from the centre.

A little further on, with the left end of **Al Warda al Hamra** now visible above, olive groves are reached left of the streambed. From there, a track goes S towards Rasoun down a steep hill. Once on the level, cross an orchard to reach a dirt track that can be seen climbing steeply towards the village. At its top, turn right onto the main road at the T-junction by the Health Centre, beyond which the RSCN Calligraphy House and Soap House are soon reached: an opportunity to support the local community.

WILD POPPIES IN AL AYOUN OLIVE GROVE

17 The Panoramic Trail
or Climbers' Path

The route starts in the hills above Wadi al Jwanieh and Rasoun, providing good views of the Ayoun area. Also known as the 'climbers path', as it passes by a number of cliffs. The walk connects a series of natural terraces along the south-facing hillside above the Ayoun valley. Pleasant walking and great views.

The route

Walk down **SW** into the trees, towards the projecting rock 'nose' that can be seen at the east end of the area's biggest cliff, **Al Warda al Hamra** (see *Climbing*), GPS alt. 860m N32° 24.688′ E35° 45.984′. Having reached the open area above the cliff top, continue **W** at about the same level with good views of Rasoun to the **S**. Shepherds' paths continue along, passing below walls, GPS alt. 870m N32° 24.585′ E35° 45.717′ then GPS alt. 875m N32° 24.583′ E35° 45.642′ before descending to a little-used narrow road just after GPS alt. 840m N32° 24.745′ E35° 45.407′, where an old rock-cut cistern might be seen – about half an hour from the end of the cliff (45mins from the start).

Go down the road for about 20m to find vague paths on the opposite side, crossing the wooded hillside to pass above old terrace walls and a small cliff (above hairpin bends in the road) known to climbers as **Shamasiyyat East Buttress** (may also be known locally as **Ergaga**), GPS alt. 825m N32° 24.712′ E35° 45.268′. (*Shamasiyyat* means 'the sunny side', referring to the south facing slopes of this hill.)

Continue at approx. the same level between small cliffs, GPS alt. 620m N32° 24.684′ E35° 45.111′ to where another climbing cliff becomes visible ahead, known as **Araq Shamasiyyat**, at GPS alt. 775m N32° 24.690′ E35° 44.983′.

VIEW FROM ABOVE AL WARDA AL HAMRA ON ROUTE 17, THE PANORAMIC TRAIL **AND ROUTE 5**, MAZAR TO RASOUN

Just below the cliff a large fallen block marks the start of a wide limestone terrace, which goes very pleasantly all the way past a small side valley to below the large cliff of **Araq Smeidah** with its 'hermit's cave' at GPS alt. 750m N32° 24.733′ E35° 44.728′. About 45mins from the last road. From there it's just a few minutes more through trees to reach the road coming up from Orjan, with the cliff of **Araq el Areadh** visible on the hillside beyond.

Return

Transport can be arranged in advance or, like us, you could hitch a ride down the road to Orjan.

GRADE
Easy walk.

DETAILS
See map on page 100. Approx. 3.5km. Though generally traversing the hillside, take care with route finding to find the easiest way as paths are not always obvious.

TIME
1½hrs–2hrs, more with stops.

APPROACH
Start at the junction of the road from Orjan with the road from Kufr Rakib to Irbid, about 4km from Orjan, see *Getting Around*. GPS alt. 900m N32° 24.917′ E35° 46.060′. The 'nose' of the cliff of Al Warda al Hamra is visible down to the right.

A NATURAL TERRACE ON ROUTE 17, THE PANORAMIC TRAIL

18 The Dolmen Trail
or Rasoun Antiquity Trail

"... Here, so close to earth's core,
   closer to the mystery of dawn
I tread softly.
Neolithic fragments
Break the skin of primal turf,
History's reminder
Should we lose our way,
Should we forget the first peoples."

Kernow, A Land Apart. Deborah King, 2002

An enjoyable and interesting 'family trail' with a viewpoint overlooking the hillside village of Rasoun, many of whose houses have been recently painted in pleasing pastels courtesy of USAID. The trail itself connects archaeological features including numerous burial chambers and dolmens, possibly dating back 5000 years, with other points of interest such as the incut floor of an ancient wine-press and water cisterns carved out of the limestone as well as the ruins of a Byzantine Church identified by its font. Handrails and steps (very anomalous in such a rural setting) have recently been fitted where deemed necessary by the Tourism Ministry in cooperation with the local community.

PLEASANT SHADE, ROUTE 18, THE DOLMEN TRAIL

The route

Walk up the sloping slab, passing the incut remains of a 'wine-press' before winding generally left up through trees eventually passing numerous ruined dolmens after which the path winds generally right to reach the viewpoint with its protective fence. Beyond that, the marked trail winds round and down the hillside to the burial caves before returning to the road beyond which the remains of a Byzantine Church are reached. The walk finishes at a specially built shelter opposite a house with a privately owned museum in its courtyard. Locally prepared food and refreshments from the village can be pre-arranged.

The Dolmen Trail is also part of a longer circular walk, which also starts in or near Rasoun, the Mar'jam Circuit.

GRADE
Easy walk. A designated 'family trail'. Though the path is well marked almost throughout, a local guide is useful to explain the sites and provide transport to the start.

DETAILS
See map on page 100. Just over 1km, starting at 830m and slowly rising to 910m before descending 200m and finishing with a short ascent.

TIME
Allow 1hr to explore the sites and enjoy the views.

APPROACH
Transport useful to reach the start of the walk, which is just over 0.5km up the steep road to Sanar above the village of Rasoun. There is a small parking area just before a hairpin bend and just beyond a sloping limestone slab on the right. GPS alt. 830m N32° 23.953′ E35° 46.200′.

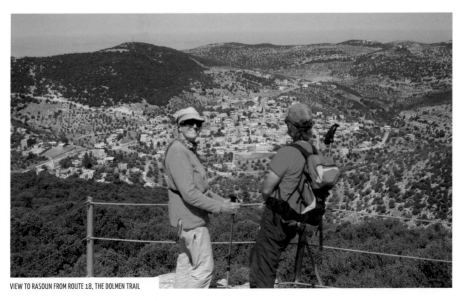

VIEW TO RASOUN FROM ROUTE 18, THE DOLMEN TRAIL

The Rasoun – Mar'jam Circuit

A very enjoyable round trip from Rasoun to Al Mar'jam and back, almost all on old tracks and finishing via the Dolmen Trail with its viewpoint and burial tombs. Short and sweet!

The route

An obvious path rises quite steeply up the left side of the valley directly ahead. After 5mins or so, the angle eases, and a pleasant green lane leads up the valley past olive groves and orchards, before reaching a house beyond which there is a small road, GPS alt. 920m N32° 23.124´ E35° 46.948´, around 1.5kms from the start (40mins).

Opposite the house, a small path will be found going up left into the woods – the key to the route. Follow it up, soon meeting a small cliff. Go right for a short distance along the foot of the cliff to find an easy way going back left through the rocks to the cliff top. Still on a shepherd's path, follow it right again, along a cliff top terrace for about 50m, after which the path zig-zags enjoyably up through the woods, eventually trending left across an open stony area, becoming more obvious again as it continues up and left between trees, GPS alt. 980m N32° 23.207´ E35° 47.063´. Continuing up, it becomes more defined, still trending left and passing below some farm buildings almost hidden in the trees (a school can also be seen from here, further up and right). Just ahead the path reaches the right side of a house, GPS alt. 1020m N32° 23.397´ E35° 46.988´, before going up right to the road in Al Mar'jam. About 1hr from the start.

Follow the road round as it bends right through the village, then turn left past a small shop (drinks etc), then left again, into a small lane at GPS alt. 1030m N32° 23.475´ E35° 47.014´, which descends to the NNW. Where it bends right, continue straight on down a steep track, which soon becomes another very pleasant green track, passing between olive groves and orchards,

TAKING A BREAK ON ROUTE 19, THE RASOUN – MAR'JAM CIRCUIT

down into a small valley. As it starts to bend left away from the valley, follow it round, first rising a little then descending as it winds round the shoulder of the hill. The path is still well defined with a retaining wall on its right, above fields, but eventually becomes a smaller path, which soon splits, at GPS alt. 900m N32° 23.769′ E35° 46.338′. Take the upper path through clearings in the trees, sometimes quite narrow, to arrive precisely at the fallen dolmens of the Dolmen Trail, GPS alt. 890m N32° 23.862′ E35° 46.206′. (If you miss the dolmens, you should still meet the Dolmen Trail, **R18** which is frequently delineated by stones placed alongside the path.) About 40mins from Mar'jam.

Follow that trail up to the viewpoint, and down to the caves, below which there is a small path. If you left a car parked at the start of the route, follow this path left above a patch of flat ground finally descending to reach the road above Ain Rasoun (the Rasoun Spring), about 200m below the starting point.

GRADE
Easy walk, though starting steeply. Take care with route finding up the wooded hillside.

DETAILS
See map on page 95. About 5.5km, dependent on choice of start and finish. If starting from the bend in the road, as described, the route starts at 800m and rises to 1030m in the village of Al Mar'jam before returning to the start with a short easy ascent along the way, on the Dolmen Trail. Alternatively, the route can start and finish at the ruined church below Rasoun, at 705m *(see R18)*.

TIME
2½hrs.

APPROACH
Though it can be started from Rasoun village, eliminating the need for transport, it's easiest to start about 1km **SE** of the village at the sharp right-hand bend on the road to Ajloun. Transport useful to reach the start. GPS alt. 800m N32° 23.506′ E35° 46.234′.

Otherwise, follow the Dolmen Trail back to Rasoun passing near the ruins of the church.

TWO VIEWS ALONG ROUTE 19, THE RASOUN – MAR'JAM CIRCUIT

The Forest & Gorge of Sirin

The clearest way into the Universe is through a forest wilderness.

John Muir

A hard day's walk with scenery varying from rural to dense forest to rocky cliff-rimmed gorges, sometimes with paths, but as the wadi descends, frequently only passable by scrambling between low hanging branches or along the stony riverbed, itself sometimes overhung by trees. Half way down, the wadi twists through giant oxbows demanding good route finding to see them at their best, then down through rocky gorges and dry waterfalls with extensive cliffs high above to finally meet the road on the upper rim of the Jordan Valley. A great adventure trek.

The route

From the building, the dirt track is followed on foot, descending gently **NE** through pleasant rural scenery, before rising up a little to meet a small lane then descending left to a farm in the valley bottom; 1km, 15mins. Now follow the farm track **NW** down the valley a short way (0.5km) and continue through fields and olive groves, always keeping near the walled streambed until a last wall is passed and the forest is entered left of the stream; 2km, 35mins from start. GPS alt. 895m N32° 25.599′ E35° 49.101′.

Continue down the thickly wooded valley with fairly frequent paths, never far from the stream, passing a path which rises left through the trees, probably to Rihaba; 3km, almost 1hr from start.

VIEW ACROSS THE OXBOWS OF ROUTE 20, THE FOREST & GORGE OF SIRIN

Another 1km further down, a road crosses the valley 1¼hr from the start. GPS alt. 850m N32° 26.159′ E35° 48.338′.

Approx. 50m to the right of the wadi bed, a path descends into the trees from the road and soon descends left to cross the valley floor and meet a wider path that also looks to start from the road about 50m left of the wadi. Follow this path and other subsequent, but intermittent paths, down through the woods, taking care to find the best way. Almost 2hrs from the start (about 5.5km) ancient terraces are passed.

Continuing down the valley for another 1.5km, with sometimes difficult going through the forest, the cliffs of **Araq Mazar** (see *Climbing* on page 87) come into view on the right after another 40mins, about 7km from the start, 2½hrs. GPS alt. 740m N32° 27.406′ E35° 47.491′. More cliffs become visible above as you reach clearings not far ahead; a nice place for a rest before plunging into ever more impenetrable woods. 1km (½hr) further on, a broad dirt track is passed. GPS alt. 720m N32° 27.703′ E35° 47.048′.

Continue down the valley still taking care with route finding, passing more cliffs then, after about 10mins, reaching a small path on the left, with cliff scenery around and ahead including one visible on the right side of the wadi, topped by horizontal limestone pavement; watch out for this path, it's the key to the route – it leads you up out of the woods and through some great wilderness scenery to the heart of the oxbows. GPS alt. 710m N32° 27.824′ E35° 46.873′.

The path goes diagonally up left to emerge on natural bedding planes of limestone pavement, opposite the ones

GRADE
Serious trek, demanding route finding skills, both in finding small shepherd's paths and in finding the high-level path through the oxbows.

DETAILS
See maps on pages 95, 98 and 99. 20km descending from almost 1000m to 200m with a couple of small ascents to cross the oxbows. Carry adequate water and use good footwear for sometimes stony terrain. Beware flash floods as the route is frequently in the wadi.

TIME
Allow 8–10hrs.

APPROACH
See *Getting around*.

seen across the wadi. Follow the bedding planes **WSW** on small paths and sheep tracks (not always obvious) to emerge in less than 0.5km almost at the crest of a rocky headland around which the first small oxbow sweeps **SE**. GPS alt. 730m N32° 27.654′ E35° 46.593′.

The second very impressive oxbow is down below, winding round its low-lying peninsula in the heart of a deep valley before heading back **NNW** then **W**. Descend carefully into the valley between small cliffs, to cross the wadi and walk up to the saddle of the peninsula, known locally as the *Rakabat* or 'neck', which is directly ahead. About 4¼hrs from start. GPS alt. 650m N32° 27.605′ E35° 46.412′. With about 9km done, and almost half way through the trek this (or the crest of the peninsula just passed) is another nice place for a break with great views around the cliff-rimmed amphitheatre. (A driveable track comes down onto the peninsula from the village of Mazar 3km to the **NE** so there may well be people there on Fridays.)

From the saddle descend steeply **W** through trees and down loose terrain into the continuation of the wadi. On the other side, sheep tracks head out along the hill-side 50m or more above the streambed, but soon lose themselves in the encroaching woods, forcing a descent into the valley bottom once more. Now almost trackless, the valley narrows to become a rocky gorge and is followed down passing a path going up left (possibly to Tibna) about 3.5km from the oxbow, GPS alt. 500m N32° 28.419′ E35° 44.541′.

Continue for about 1.5km with occasional cliffs on either side of the wadi and increasingly large cliffs above, some with intriguing cave-like entrances. The going is frequently in the streambed, which has numerous small, hopefully dry waterfalls until the first olive groves are met, sometimes offering easier walking than the stony streambed. Further down, more olive groves are passed as the wadi becomes more open and the trees disappear. 15mins or so further on, a track is passed which zig-zags up left to reach the road to Tibna, GPS alt. 320m N32° 29.655′ E35° 43.827′. 2km further down the now open valley, after passing some beehives (take care!) the path reaches the Tibna road, which is now in the valley bottom, GPS alt. 235m N32° 30.185′ E35° 42.660′ (approx. 8hrs). From there it's just over 1km down the road to the main road along the rim of the Jordan Valley.

Return

Pre-arrange a vehicle to Al Ayoun, Pella, or your chosen destination.

LOOKING ALONG THE OXBOWS IN WADI SIRIN

FOLLOWING THE DRY STREAM BED IN THE FORESTED DEPTHS OF WADI SIRIN

> Climb if you will, but remember that courage and strength are nought without prudence and that a momentary negligence may destroy the happiness of a lifetime. Do nothing in haste, look well to each step and from the beginning think what may be the end.

Scrambles Amongst the Alps, Edward Whymper, 1871

ROCK **CLIMBING**

Important

"*Fixed anchors, where appropriate, must be substantially unnoticeable and must not have a significant adverse impact on the primeval character and influence of the wilderness area*".

From '***Climbing and Fixed Anchors in the Wilderness***', Climbing magazine, USA, May 1994.

DETAILS
See map on page 100 for all cliff locations.

Traditional protection was used on all the following routes except *Fingery Wall* and *Surprise Wall* on Araq Damaj, which have no natural protection and were top roped. **Please place fixed gear sparingly and not where traditional gear can be used.** In this way, people can learn how to place protection before attempting the big adventure climbs in Rum and elsewhere. As the Norwegian Alpine Club says, aim at preserving the potential for adventurous climbing for future generations of climbers – acquire the necessary equipment and skills instead of using fixed gear. This is the only way to ensure the full, unspoilt adventure, remains for everybody to explore, and not just for the first ascentionists. Keep it clean!

The cliffs, which are all limestone, are described from south to north, the first being beneath Mar Elyas *(see R4 and R6)*.

CLIMBING EISA'S DEBUT, ARAQ KHALET HEMED

Araq Khalet Hemed

This **S** facing cliff has easy access, is in a
nice location and has the usual good rock,
though it is generally less steep than other
local cliffs, offering climbs for beginners
and having natural protection (nuts,
slings and cams) as well as possibilities
for bolder, more technical problems.
We first visited here in March 2010 with
Eisa Dweekat (see *Contacts* on page 102).

Approach

When driving through Ishtafeina in the
direction of Al Ayoun (see *Getting to Al
Ayoun*), turn left at the sign for Mar Elyas,
then turn right just before the final hill to
the antiquity site. Follow the road as it
contours round the hill of Mar Elyas and
descends right to near the old mosque
at Listib. Just beyond, the crag is visible
down to the **NW** on the right side of
the small valley of Wadi Khalet Hemed,
and left of the ridge, about 0.5km away.
Either park off-road near the old mosque
at Listib and walk **W** down the hillside to
reach the cliff in 10mins, or drive down
a rough little road to the left then fork
right and park near the end of the track,
opposite the right end of the cliff, which is
just across the little wooded valley at GPS
alt. 685m N32° 22.011′ E35° 42.739′.
There are two cliffs, the **Western Cliff**,
which has a few possibilities, and to
it's right:

The Main Cliff

Starting from the left, the obvious vertical
crack gives a steep start to the day:

1 **Prickly Crack** *   8m   5
  Climb direct.

About 50m to the right, the steepening
ridge with small pinnacles at its base is:

2 **Bristly Ridge** *   10m   2+
  Climb direct, keeping to the ridge.

Right again, past a tree, there is a very nice
pocketed buttress with two faces divided
by a pointed boulder at the base; its left
wall is climbed delicately by:

3 **Eisa's Debut** ***   8m   5-
  Delightfully up the centre of the face.

Further right, the cliff is more broken until
just before the end there is a buttress with
a prominent left-facing corner on its left:

4 **Layback Crack** *   8m   3
  Easy rocks lead to the nice wide
  layback crack.

Or, more boldy:

5 **Layback Arête** *   8m   5
  Climb up to the first foothold on the
  right wall of the layback crack, then
  move delicately right to layback the
  arête to the top. Exposed.

The next cliff, Araq Damaj, is about 1km
away, almost due **N** over the shoulder of
the hill in Wadi Listib (see *R7*), and easily
reached from Baoun.

NINE YEAR OLD GABRIEL KHANO GETS TO GRIPS WITH EISA'S DEBUT, ARAQ KHALET HEMED

Araq Damaj

A spectacular **S** facing cliff with potential for hard equipped routes, but mostly hidden from view until you reach it. Both sectors are in a beautiful location above the tree filled gorge of Wadi Listib with views towards Wadi Yabis and the Jordan Valley in the **W** and with the hills of Mar Elyas and Listib opposite. 15–20m in height and good quality limestone; the cliffs are reached in 5mins from the road, the **W** (right hand cliff when looking from the road) is at GPS alt. 550m N32° 22.599′ E35° 42.780′.

There are rock terraces below both sectors, that under the **W** being about 4m or so above a much larger grassy terrace, which can be walked with ease (the upper one is also easy though narrow in places). The first climbs here and on all the following cliffs, unless otherwise mentioned, were done in March 2009, together with Mark Khano of *Guiding Star/Sarha* (see *Appendix*) and Mick Shaw, a regular member of our 'nomads' team.

Opposite Araq Damaj, the 20m high wave-shaped cliff on the south side of

TONY HOWARD FEELS HIS WAY UP FINGERY WALL, ARAQ DAMAJ

Wadi Listib is **Araq al Hamra**. There is no climbing there as the cliff is capped by a 6m roof, but abseiling off the top is fun, and a hole high in the cliff looks an intriguing objective.

Approach

From the Baoun junction on the main road from Ishtafeina, go down the hill for 1km to GPS alt. 620m N32° 23.119′ E35° 42.858′. Here, the main road bends down right and the Ausara road continues ahead. Follow it for 1.5km then turn up left and follow a steep gravel lane for another 1km to reach a parking area at the top of the hill and at the end of a metal fence, GPS alt. 660m N32° 22.719′ E35° 42.861′. **Araq al Hamra** is visible across the valley to the S and the edge of **Araq Damaj West buttress** can be seen down to the right.

From the parking place, scramble easily down the hillside keeping left of the fence until it turns abruptly right. The two sectors of **Araq Damaj** are now visible below, to the left and right.

Alternative Approach

Turn left off the main road just beyond the fourth turn on the right coming down the road from Ishtafeina, and just before a bent pine on the left, at GPS alt. 680m N32° 23.055′ E35° 43.465′. Drive up the short steep hill then contour along the increasingly rough road **S**, then steeply down and up past pines to a T-junction, turn right (**WNW**) and continue, passing left of a house to the parking place just before the point where the road passes between metal fences (*see above*).

Western Sector

This is a fine cliff of grey limestone, quite long, with a 'cave' near the left end. Apart from a few climbs at its extreme right end, where the angle eases, all routes will be steep and difficult and require professional equipping. The right end of the cliff starts with a nice grey wall with a huge block on its top right:

1   **Intro Wall**   15m   2
    Follow good holds up from bottom
    right to finish left of the huge block.

8m lower down there is a small scoop in the wall with a flat stone on the ground below; 3m above, a small 'finger' of rock points skywards. To its right is:

2   **Fingery Wall**   20m   5-
    Climb the right arête of the scoop then
    delicately up the wall above. No pro.

3   **The Fickle Finger** *   20m   5
    Move up and left to reach the finger,
    then straight up passing right of a short
    crack.

4   **Time's Up**   20m   4
    Climb the left arête of the scoop then
    straight up passing left of a short crack.

Eastern Sector

The left end of this sector begins with an arête immediately left of a tree in a gully:

5   **The Ridge**   12m   3
    Gain the arête and climb it pleasantly
    to the top, with the start of the next
    route directly opposite across the head
    of the gully.

Right of the belay at the top of the previous climb there is an obvious steep wall with a hollow in its centre:

6 **Surprise Wall** *   12m   5+
Climb directly to the basin then up the walls above to a tree belay. No pro.

To reach the next route, traverse right along the ledge beneath the overhanging cliff to reach another tree in a gully at the foot of the cliff. Immediately right a 2m wide ridge goes directly to the top, cut by an almost horizontal crack 2m below the top.

7 **The Pillar**   20m   5+
Up the ridge, which steepens to committing final moves on the left edge; smallish wires, a couple of slings and a cam 2–4 in the break below the top.

Moving **N**, there are a number of cliffs on both sides of and above upper Wadi Yabis (Wadi Rayyan), 2km west of Baoun. Most will be seen by driving up alongside the wadi to Baoun from Oudeh watermill (see *R2, Getting around*). The upper cliffs are easily accessible from Baoun; approaching from this direction, the first is **Ras el Qasr**, some towers and cliffs, max. 8m high perched high above the wadi, GPS alt. 610m N32° 23.549′ E35° 42.955′. **SE** of there, down a ravine and across the head of a narrow valley is the wave-like cliff of **Organ Suweid** with its inaccessible cave. Opposite and down below there are more cliffs on both sides of the valley, around 10–15m high, some vegetated, some with cave-like holes and overhangs and climbing possibilities. Mahmoud Hawawreh (see *Contacts*) visited this area with us.

The red cliff of **Organ al Rahiban** is further up the wadi, on its north side, opposite Orjan. The rock is poor quality but it's known for its 'Hermits' Caves' and is easily accessed by car, GPS alt. 590m N32° 24.009′ E35° 43.765′.

ABSEILING AT ARAQ DAMAJ

The next cliff is above the road from Baoun to Orjan.

Araq en Nahleh

The cliff is never more than 10m high, but is good rock and faces **SW** in a nice location above Baoun at GPS alt. 810m N32° 23.167′ E35° 44.276′.

Approach

From the shops opposite the café in Baoun, two small cliffs can be seen above the wooded hillside to the **NE**. The cliffs are almost directly above the road as it bends round the wadi heading from Baoun to Orjan. Turn right before the wadi and drive a short way up before turning left over the wadi to park higher up, just beyond a couple of houses, then head up the wooded hillside to the cliffs (10mins).

There are no climbs yet on the bigger, right hand cliff, the only route to date being on the left:

| **Gabriel** | 6m | 4 |

Up the 3m lower wall and the steep crack above. Pleasant.

The next five cliffs are ranged along the hillside about 3km **N** of Orjan. The first is Araq el Areadh. All can be visited in a day via The Climbers' Path, **R17**.

Araq el Areadh

The **SE** facing cliff, which is generally around 10–20m high and good rock, can be seen from the road below, as you drive up from Orjan.

Approach

See *Getting around: Getting to treks, caves and cliffs north of Al Ayoun.* Driving **NNE** from Orjan for about 3km, and immediately before the T-junction at the top of the hill, GPS alt. 810m, N32° 24.888′ E35° 44.587′, turn left onto a small lane and follow it until it becomes a grass track in 200m or so. Walking left above orchards soon brings you to the cliff top above the:

Eastern Sector

This part of the cliff is rarely more than 5m high, but follow the cliff top right for 5mins or so, past a break in the cliff, to a way down almost at the far end of the:

Western Sector

Once down below the cliff, a few more buttresses can be seen further on. The first has a wave-profile common in this area but is too small to be of interest. The ones beyond are even smaller. However, to the left (**E**) of the descent, looking down, there is much of interest on excellent rock. All routes were climbed using traditional protection. GPS alt. 770m N32° 24.630′ E35° 44.293′.

The crag is initially about 10m high and has three obvious grooves, the first and shortest starts from a cave, but hasn't been climbed. The middle groove, which had a discarded snakeskin in the first handhold, is:

| 1 | **Snakeskin Corner** | 10m | 4- |

A tricky start leads to easier, but razor sharp rock.

The right hand groove is just left of a 3m prow and gives the even more rasping:

MICK SHAW LEADING THE FIRST ASCENT OF THE JABBERWORK, ARAQ EL AREADH

2   Cheesegrater *   10m   5

Enter the groove and move right to
the parallel crack, which is bridged
to the summit rock.

About 25m further right along the foot of
the buttress is a big grey wall above a 5m
lower tier. This is the biggest and best part
of the cliff, with one route to date starting
below the large block at the bottom right
of the wall:

3   The Jabberwock ***   20m   6a

*"Beware the Jabberwock, my son
The claws that catch the teeth that
bite"...*
Lewis Carrol, Through the Looking Glass.

Climb the lower tier directly to the left
side of the block. Gain the wall above
and climb a shallow groove until it's
possible to make an exposed but nice
traverse left to reach a plaque of rock
projecting slightly from the face. Above
is the crux: climb the steep groove right
of the plaque to gain the hanging crack,
which slants left to the top. Carry a
selection of wires and micro-cams and
a sling for the plaque.

Other possibilities exist nearby, some of
which could be climbed 'clean' without
fixed gear, but at the moment the only
other climb is well to the E, where two
small buttresses will eventually be reached.
The second one has a nice rounded rib
with hollows on its right:

4   The Grey Rib   8m   3

Pleasantly up the rib on razor-sharp holds.

Even further on through bushes, the
Eastern Sector is reached again, offering
some short problems before returning
easily and directly back to the track
and parking place. The hillside E of here,
across the main road is predominantly
S facing and is known locally as
Shamasiyyat (Sunny Side). A number
of cliffs continue along the hillside at a
similar level to the previous crag, and can
be visited in a day walking along *R17,
The Panoramic Trail, or Climbers Path*,
which is described E to W.

Going the opposite way along the cliffs,
approaching by road from Orjan, the first
cliff is Araq Smeideh.

Araq Smeideh

A S facing cliff of good rock 15–20m high,
with some climbing possibilities on the
extensive wall left of the large 'Hermit's
Cave' reached in 5mins from the road,
GPS alt. 750m N32° 24.733′ E35° 44.728′.

Approach

As for Araq er Areadh *(see above)*, but
park left of the road opposite a pylon and
level with the crag, which is obvious to the
right and easily reached though trees.

One route was climbed by us in March
2010, up an obvious curved crack splitting
the first steep buttress about 50m in from
the left end of the cliff. The buttress has a
protruding nose of rock at its top, about
5m to the right of the crack and there is a
1.5m square boulder on the ground, also
about 5m to the right. Start in trees below
the crack:

DI TAYLOR HAS FUN IN THE SUN, **ARAQ SMEIDAH**

Fun in the Sun ✳✳✳   15m   5
Climb the pocketed wall to the crack, which gives delightful climbing, first by laybacks, then bridging. Good pro from small–medium wires and cams.

The next cliff is 5mins walk along the hillside. Having no special local name, we called it after the hill, Araq Shamasiyyat.

Araq Shamasiyyat

Located at GPS alt. 775m N32° 24.690′ E35° 44.983′, the cliff is about 15m high but not as extensive as **Araq Smeideh**. Three climbs were discovered by us in March 2010, all protectable with trad gear (cams, slings and nuts), and there are a few harder unclimbed possibilities.

Approach

From the ledge below the Hermit's Cave at **Araq Smeidah**, descend 5m to the next ledge down and follow the terrace E contouring along past the mouth of a small valley to arrive at the crag, identified by a large fallen block at its foot, after about 5mins (**R17** in reverse).

The first climb is immediately left of the oak tree growing on a ledge in the centre of the cliff:

1   Oak Tree Corner ✳   13m   4+
Climb the lower wall directly to the corner or climb pockets below the tree to gain the same ledge. Continue up the corner and finish via the short headwall.

Next is the obvious crack right of the tree, which provided the first route on the cliff:

2   English Breakfast   15m   5-
Gain the crack, climb it steeply, then move right round the arête, taking care with fragile rock to finish up the final crack of the next route:

3   Hanging Groove ✳✳   13m   5
Pull into the overhanging groove right of the arête and climb it steeply, pulling out on rounded prickly holds to reach the final crack.

Heading E again (**R17** in reverse), the next cliff is another 5mins further on at GPS alt. 805m N32° 24.689′ E35° 45.109′, but has no climbs of real interest. A similar distance beyond, the fourth cliff is reached, just before a hairpin bend in a roughly surfaced road, coming up from Wadi Orjan.

Ergaga (Shamasiyyat East Buttress)

This **S** facing cliff, which is just **W** of the hairpin bend in the old road is above GPS alt. 760m N32° 24.670′ E35° 45.310′ and can be seen when looking across from the valley **W** of Rasoun. It is about 20m high in places, but very broken and partially concealed by bushes.

Approach

As for Araq er Areadh *(see above)*, turning right at the top of the hill, then right again after 1.5km to go down a steep rough road to some hairpin bends. The crag is to the right.

Alternative Approach

Instead of crossing Wadi Orjan after leaving Orjan, follow it up a short way then cross the wadi and drive up the same hillside on the next (very steep and rough) road to the E, to a big layby on a hairpin bend almost at the top.

The large slab on the right of the cliff has a nice easy climb:

Fluted Slab   20m   3+

Up the centre of the slab on fluted holds, passing right of the overhang to gain the finishing groove. Initially climbed solo – protection is scarce.

The next and most impressive cliff is **E** again, still at a similar level, opposite and 1.5km **N** of Rasoun; Al Warda al Hamra.

Al Warda al Hamra
(also known as Al Thôr al Ahmar)

The cliff extends about 300m and faces generally **S**, mostly 20–30m in height. It is unrelentingly steep with numerous overhangs though there are some possibilities for routes to be climbed without fixed equipment, particularly cracks *(see below)*.

Interestingly the letters M and A have been scratched into the rock above a ledge about half way up the face and maybe half way along the main cliff. Close inspection reveals a hole through the roof of the cliff above the right end of the ledge. We located this at the top of the cliff and it would be possible to abseil through the hole to the ledge then continue down to the ground. Strange that whoever did this doesn't seem to have left any trace of climbing and nobody in Al Ayoun knows of any climbers having visited the area prior to us.

CLIMBING THE FIRST TASTE AT AL WARDA AL HAMRA, RASOUN IN THE BACKGROUND

INITIAL EXPLORATION, AL WARDA AL HAMRA

Approach

As for **R17** (see *Getting around*) then walk directly down a field to enter the trees about level with the rock nose before heading rightwards towards it, descending slightly to find a shepherd's path which leads to the base of the cliff just beyond, GPS alt. 840m N32° 24.759′ E35° 45.858′.

One route was climbed by us in March 2010, approaching from the top on good ledges to where a metal spike (purpose unknown) has been hammered into the ground about 80m right of the projecting nose. We abseiled in 5m right of this to the bottom of two wide parallel cracks either side of a narrow pillar. The cracks start from a wooded terrace about 7m up from the foot of the crag and before the next red overhangs start as you walk along the bottom 80m after the nose. Seen from the top, the route is almost opposite the left end of an olive grove in the valley below:

The First Taste   20m   5-
Start just right of the right crack, which overhangs slightly at its base. Pull up and step across to follow the crack steeply before climbing its right wall to the top. Assorted cams and slings useful.

Visible from here, 1km to the E, across the wadi, is Araq Sharaf.

Araq Sharaf
The **W** facing cliff extends about 200m and is steep and perfect grey limestone 7–10m high with obvious climbing potential, but no routes yet.

Approach
On the **SE** side of Rasoun, turn left onto a small road signed Sanar into a valley with ancient olive groves on the left concealing the ruins of a small church (see **R18**). Continue steeply up the hill turning left 1.5km from Rasoun, after a hairpin bend, onto a gravel road signed to '*Rasoun Tourist Camp*' with a house on its left. Turn left again after 0.3km then left again onto a rough track after 100m. After 300m on this track ask permission to park at the campsite in trees on the crest of the hill, then walk down left for 100m to arrive at the top of the highest point of the cliff, GPS alt. 910m N32° 24.222′ E35° 46.074′. Seen from Rasoun, the cliff reappears further N but we have not yet had chance to take a look.

The next cliff was seen when trekking through Wadi Sirin (R20). Not knowing it's name we have called it after the village.

Araq Mazar

This is a steep and extremely extensive cliff, 15–20m in height and over 400m long, with considerable potential for climbing. The S facing **Western Sector** has not been visited yet but can be seen when looking right from the car park, whilst the top of the **Main Cliff**, which is W facing, is just below and about 50m away. We made a brief visit in April 2010 with Mark Khano of *Guiding Star/Sarha* (see *Appendix*).

Approach

From the centre of Mazar, shops and small café, (see *R5* and *R20, Getting to treks, caves and cliffs north of Al Ayoun*), drive **SW** on the left side of the village for about 200m until a small road goes steeply down left soon after a large building. Follow this for just over 1km until a cliff top is seen just below the right side of the road, and above the deep, winding wooded valley of Wadi Sirin (R20). There is a parking place on the left, near some pines, at GPS 820m N32° 27.402′ E35° 47.597′ and another one on the right of the road a little further on.

The Main Cliff

Descending directly from the first car park gains access to the left end of the cliff but the climbing potential is less at this end, and there is a depressing amount of litter that has been thrown over the cliff by picnickers (so probably best to avoid Fridays). The best part of the cliff is further right and litter-free being further from the road. To reach the right end walk left along the cliff top for about 300m to a wall, just beyond which a well-used path descends rocks to the foot of the crag. If you park at the second car park, descend diagonally left to reach the wall.

From the right end of the cliff, walk below the crag for about 25m to below an overhanging buttress partially concealed by trees, with an overhanging crack on its left. Another 15m further on there is another overhanging buttress with a hanging chimney on its left. 10m after that a tree grows from the cliff with a thin crack rising steeply up the wall on its left and a large block at its foot:

Temptation ✳✳   15m   5
Gain the crack from the right, and climb it nicely before trending left on improving holds up the headwall. Small to medium wires and cams.

There are numerous possible routes on this cliff, some trad, but mostly sports climbs. Enjoy!

CAVING

Caving in Jordan is in its infancy, but there is potential for more discoveries around Al Ayoun. Much of the area is Wadi Sir Dolomitic limestone from the late Cretaceous Period (80–94 million years old), faults generally running **WNW-ESE**. Working from **S** to **N**, the first possible cave is on the cliff of **Araq al Hamra** where there is an obvious hole high in the cliff, but difficult of access due to the wave-profile of the crag and the 6m overhang above the hole. An abseil in the correct place should determine whether or not the hole leads anywhere (see *Climbing* on page 77 and photo, page 91).

Moving north, there is a similarly intriguing hole in the cliff of **Organ Suweid** (see *Climbing* on page 78). The **Cave of Abu Salih** (to which Abu Salih reputedly eloped with his girlfriend, living there with her until they were allowed to marry) is lower down the hillside. Mahmoud Hawawreh (see *Contacts*) knows the locations. Moving **N** again, the first pothole to be discovered in Jordan is about 3km north of Al Ayoun. A pothole is a water-eroded vertical cave in the rock, rather than a horizontal passage. We found it quite by chance in thick forest, whilst exploring Wadi el Hawi in 2009 for trekking possibilities, and returned a week later with Mahmoud Hawawreh.

Having talked to a local farmer, he told us that three French people had been down the pothole in 2008, so we were not the first to explore it.

Cave Conservation

Prof Stephan Kempe, a member of a survey of Birqish Cave (also known as Al Daher Cave or Zubia Cave) in Dec 2006, asked us to point out that "The problem with giving locations of caves is rather grave since people are digging everywhere and destroying very valuable scientific resources. In Al-Daher, flowstone is being removed and there is no way to stop it. Please point out the absolute need for conservative visitation only; may I also recommend that anybody who is defacing this or other caves in Jordan, damaging their interior or even stealing objects, should be reported to the authorities."

In October 2009, experienced caver, Carlos Abellanosa, reported considerable damage to the Birqish cave, with graffiti and litter both outside and in. Together with students from the King's Academy, Amman, they removed 71kgs of litter. They have suggested that a securely locked gate should be fitted, with a key held by local people, together with education about the environmental importance of caves.

El Hawi Pothole

The pothole is an intriguing discovery; it's only about 1km from Birqish Cave, which is itself only 1km from the Ain Zubia resurgence so a good cave system may yet be discovered in this area. Vertical shafts as big as El Hawi, which is over 25m deep and exhibits some cave formations such as speleotherms and boxwork (both noted by Carlos Abellanosa), usually lead to subterranean water-worn passages, unless they are just isolated solution pockets. There is a widening chamber at the bottom of the shaft but if any passages exist, they are choked by soil and stones that have fallen down the hole over the millennia. Carlos Abellanosa has spent time down there and a lot of digging would almost certainly be needed to have any chance of discovering an ongoing cave system. For a country with no other major potholes, the 23m abseil in is a uniquely foreboding experience and the Prussik out is good exercise!

GRADE
Serious cave, grade 3, due to the long vertical shaft, the sides of which overhang almost throughout, making technical equipment and skills indispensable; **do not enter without them**.

DETAILS
50m of rope is plenty (low stretch is preferable and two are useful) plus abseil and Prussik gear and, of course, helmets and head torches. There is some loose rock in the shaft wall, so take care.

APPROACH
See *Getting to treks, caves and cliffs north of Al Ayoun*, as for *R12 Judeita Trail*, but only following the lane down for about 1.5km to the valley bottom, GPS alt. 740m N32° 25.646′ E35° 44.531′, with olive groves on the left and a small building just ahead, also on the left, with a parking space opposite. If the farmer is there, ask permission to park and leave space for other cars. It was this helpful, friendly man that told us about the French visitors. With his permission, walk down through the farmland taking care of crops and walls, to enter the forest close to the valley bottom (where a stream would be if there ever was one). The hole should be found a little further on through the trees and a few metres left of the streambed. Around 5 mins (300m) from the road. GPS alt. 715m N32° 25.604′ E35° 44.402′.

RETURNING FROM THE DEPTHS OF EL HAWI POTHOLE

To date, the best known, largest and most complex cave in Jordan is:

Birqish Cave
(also known as Al Daher Cave or Zubia Cave)

The cave is in a beautiful location in an area of karst limestone and Mediterranean-type hill country, above the Zubia Valley (see *R13*) at an altitude of 800m. It is (or was, see above) well decorated with cave formations. It is also a refuge for bats and people once made use of it (we found some ancient pottery inside, which we gave to an archaeologist).

GRADE
Easy cave.

DETAILS
Full details are in our guide to *Jordan – Walks, Treks, Caves, Climbs and Canyons (R145)*. We have been told the army and local people have now made the access to the cave easier to encourage visitors. Apparently they blasted the entrance so a rope-aided descent into the cave is no longer necessary. Also what was a crawl into the main chamber through a narrow passage has gone. As a result the cave, which was once used by early man is now full of litter. Stals and other cave features have been smashed and the roof is blackened by smoke, destroying what was, not long ago, a pristine cave and home to bats and other cave creatures. It's an ecological disaster.

It has been rightly suggested that the cave should be locked to protect it. If you go, respect the cave environment and the bats and other creatures that live there and please do not damage any remaining formations. For a full professional report and topo, see the *Journal of Cave & Karst Studies, Dec 06, v.68*, no. 3, p.107-114, found via the link: **www.caves.org/pub/journal/Journal_of_Cave_and_Karst_Studies_volume_68.htm**

APPROACH
Since first writing about this cave in the mid nineties there have been many changes to the landscape between the road and the cave and new walls and houses have been built. For anyone still interested in going see *Getting to treks, caves and cliffs north of Al Ayoun*, as for **R15**. Park near GPS alt. 836m N32º 26.185′ E35º 44.493′ at any off-road spot that doesn't impede traffic. Follow the wall left of the new house on the **N** side of the road then descend slightly right then left to reach the cave in 5 mins. GPS alt. 817m N32º 26.212′ E35º 44.640′.

DI TAYLOR IN BIRQISH CAVE

Down below in the forested valley of Zubia are:

Ain Zubia Caves

The two small cave entrances are the location of a spring and were full of water when we visited, and when Carlos Abellanosa explored a little further into the sumps. Their location is intriguing as Birqish Cave is about 170m above and less than 1km away.

We are not aware of any caves north of here, but there is said to be an underground church in Wadi Taiyiba (**R10**). There is also an interesting report on '*Chalcolithic caves discovered east of the River Jordan*', by Jaimie L. Lovell, Director of the Kenyon Institute, see: **www.antiquity.ac.uk/projgall/lovell322/**

DETAILS

The two adjacent cave entrances are each about 1m wide and 1.5m high. The one on the left is square-cut and appears man-made; it goes about 14m in 30cm deep water before the cave roof slopes down to meet the water, barring progress. The cave on the right goes about 20m before the same situation occurs. Unlike the left hand one, this seems to be a natural cave, which becomes quite wide before the cave roof submerges under the water. Just inside the entrance, a man-made wall divides this passage from a small running stream, which disappears almost immediately. The caves may be of historical or cultural interest – perhaps the Water Authority or someone studying hydrology may know more about them?

APPROACH

The caves are about 3km, 1hr, from the start of **R13** but not worth a special visit.

ABSEIL OVER ARAQ AL HAMRA CLIFF TO CHECK A POSSIBLE CAVE ENTRANCE

Area Maps

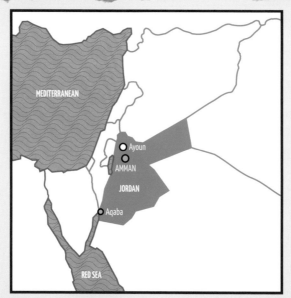

Middle East

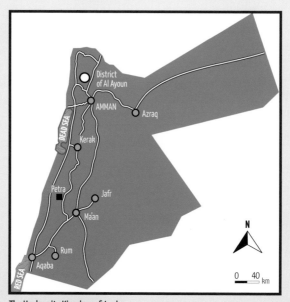

The Hashemite Kingdom of Jordan

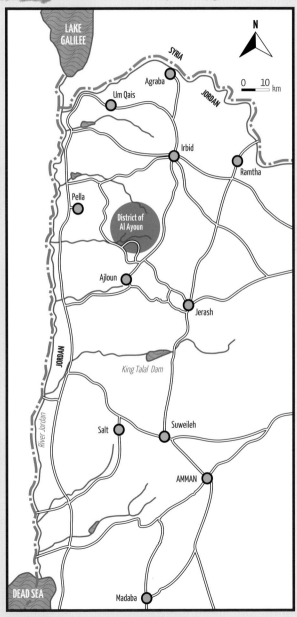

LAKE GALILEE

SYRIA

JORDAN

N

0   10 km

Agraba

Um Qais

Irbid

Ramtha

Pella

District of
Al Ayoun

Ajloun

Jerash

King Talal Dam

River Jordan

JORDAN

Salt

Suweileh

AMMAN

DEAD SEA

Madaba

The Jordan Valley, Al Ayoun & the Northern Highlands

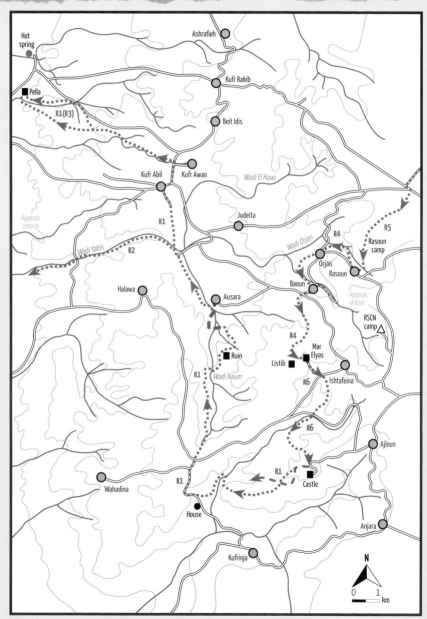

Ajloun to Pella walks & treks – Routes 1, 2, 3, 4, 5, 6

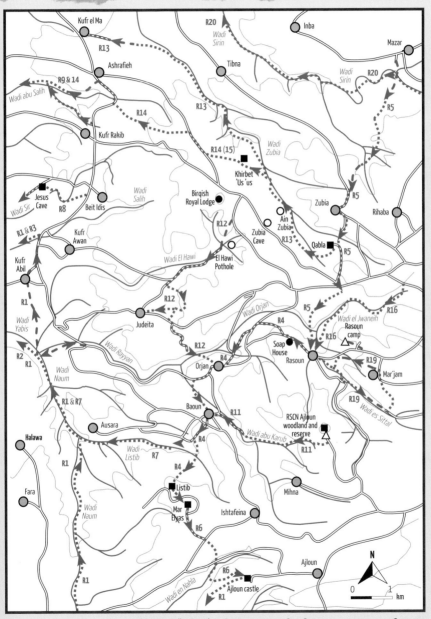

Al Ayoun walks & treks – Routes 1, 2, 4, 5, 6, 7, 8, 9, 11, 12, 13, 14, 15, 16, 19, 20

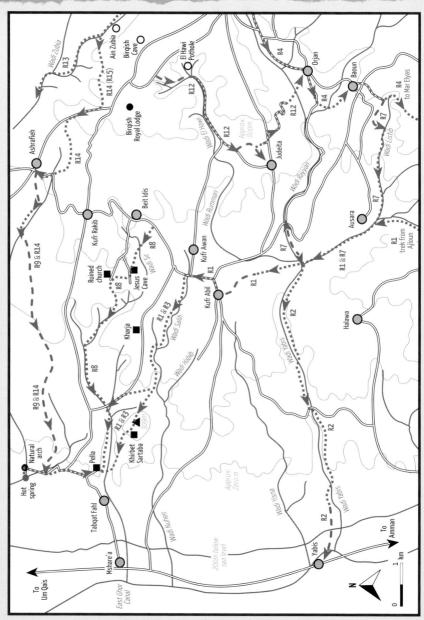

Al Ayoun, Yabis & Pella walks & treks – Routes 1, 2, 3, 4, 7, 9, 12, 13, 14, 15

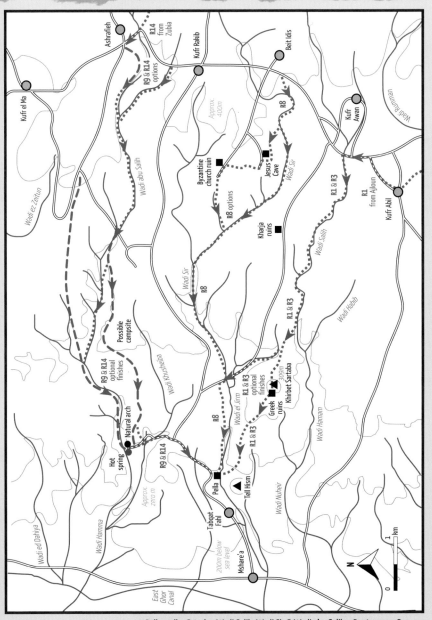

Pella walks & treks: Wadi Salih, Wadi Sir & Wadi abu Salih – Routes 1, 3, 8, 9, 14

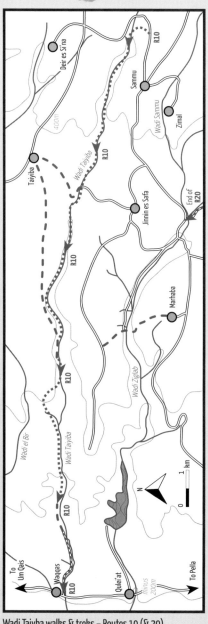

Wadi Taiyba walks & treks – Routes 10 (& 20)

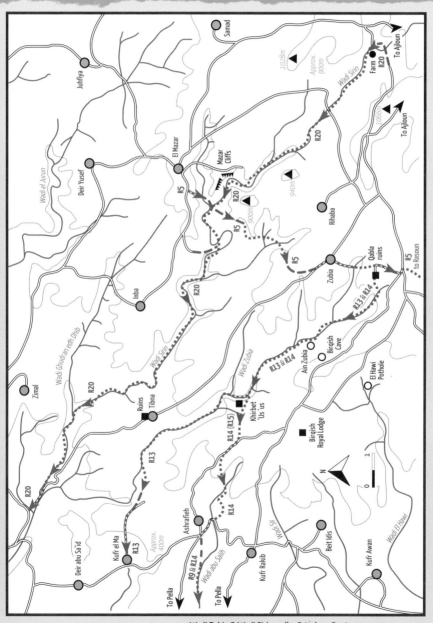

Wadi Zubia & Wadi Sirin walks & treks – Routes 5, 9, 13, 14, 15, 20

Area Maps

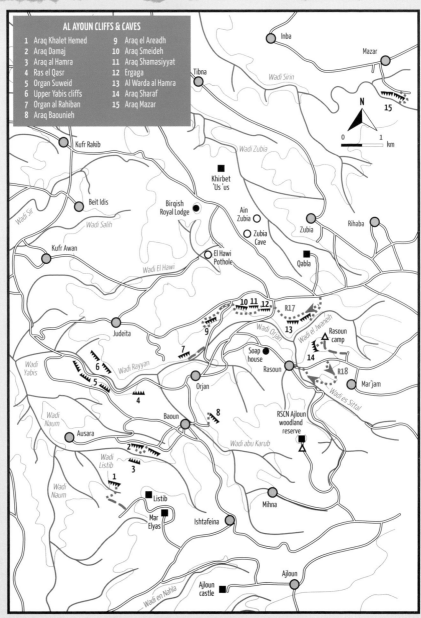

AL AYOUN CLIFFS & CAVES

1	Araq Khalet Hemed	9	Araq el Areadh
2	Araq Damaj	10	Araq Smeideh
3	Araq al Hamra	11	Araq Shamasiyyat
4	Ras el Qasr	12	Ergaga
5	Organ Suweid	13	Al Warda al Hamra
6	Upper Yabis cliffs	14	Araq Sharaf
7	Organ al Rahiban	15	Araq Mazar
8	Araq Baounieh		

Al Ayoun cliffs & caves – Routes 17, 18, cliffs & caves

Appendix

And the end of all our exploring will be to arrive where we started and know the place for the first time.

T S Elliot

Accommodation in & around Al Ayoun

The Ayoun Community Project is considering converting old houses to a lodge for visitors as well as a campsite overlooking the valley of Al Ayoun. The person to contact for updates on this project or for home-stay and/or meals in the villages is the ex-Mayor, Mohammed abu Ibrahim *(contact below)*. In 2011, home-stay cost 20JD, B & B. Lunch and evening meal both around 12JD dependent on requirements. Don't miss a home-cooked Al Ayoun meal, they are superb.

The RSCN Ajloun Woodland Reserve is in the hills above and has cabin accommodation. They also have a small lodge at their Biscuit House below Orjan. Contact:

RSCN Headquarters
T: 00962 (0)6461 6523
E: tourism@rscn.jo
www.rscn.org.jo

On the opposite side of the Ayoun valley, the **Rasoun Tourist Camp** is located on a high headland looking S over Rasoun, contact:

Zuher al Share
T: 00962 (0)7979 30071 or
    00962 (0)7769 94709
E: zuhershare@gmail.com
www.rasouncamp.com

Further afield, there are a couple of hotels in Ajloun, the **Al Rabad Castle hotel**, T: 02 642 0202, and the **Ajloun Hotel**, T: 02 642 0524, both around 40JD/double B & B but rather run-down. The much better **Olive Branch Resort** is between Ajloun and Jerash, so around a ½hr from Al Ayoun by car (see *Getting Around, Getting to Al Ayoun the quick way*). Rooms are 50JD/double B & B, with camping at 11JD/person (rates reduce by 10% discount for extra nights).

Olive Branch Resort
T: 00962 (0)2634 0555/00962 (0)7955 23546
E: olivekh@go.com.jo
www.olivebranch.com.jo

If planning to stay overnight in Pella in the Jordan valley, where some of the treks end, contact:

Dib Hussein
Pella Rest House Manager and proprietor of the **Pella Countryside Hotel**, 40JD/double B & B, evening meal no extra cost.
M: 0795 574 145 and 0776 184 337
E: dheebjawahreh575@hotmail.com

Finally, we should mention that there is a huge tourism development project planned for the whole Ajloun/Al Ayoun area, including new hotels, so let's hope this enhances the area and doesn't detract from grass-roots local projects.

Contacts

All visitors to Al Ayoun needing further information, assistance, accommodation, guides or help with transport are requested to contact the following in advance of their visit:

Mohammed abu Ibrahim

Al Ayoun Tourism Coordinator
M: 0777 765 881
E: mohdswalmeh@live.com

Eisa Dweekat

Director, Orjan area/
Al Ayoun municipality
M: 0796 829 111
E: eisa_dweekat73@yahoo.com

Mahmoud Hawawreh

Retired English teacher
M: 0777 072 212
E: mahmoud_hawawreh@yahoo.com

For information on Pella and antiquity sites in the surrounding hills, and for accommodation or help with transport in the Pella area, contact:

Dib Hussein

M: 0795 574 145 and
   0776 184 337
E: dheebjawahreh575@hotmail.com

Jordanian adventure tourism operators working in Al Ayoun:

Discovery
www.discovery1.com

Petra Moon
www.petramoon.com

Sarha
www.sarha.jo

Terhaal
www.terhaal.com

Tropical Desert
www.tropicaldeserttrips.com

Based in England but operating pilgrim tours in the Middle East:

Wider Horizons
www.wider-horizons.org

Based in Palestine & Jordan:

Guiding Star
www.guidingstarltd.com

Other useful websites

Ruwwad
Co-founded by Fadi Ghandour,
the sponsor of this book
www.ruwwad.jo

RSCN
(Royal Society for the
Conservation of Nature)
www.rscn.org.jo

Walking Jordan
www.walkingjordan.com

Desert Guides
www.desertguides.com

Ruth's Jordan
www.jordanjubilee.com

Abraham's Path
www.abrahampath.org

The authors
www.nomadstravel.co.uk

Associated reading

Walks in Palestine and The Nativity Trail,
2001, Di Taylor & Tony Howard,
Cicerone Press

*Jordan – Walks, Treks, Caves,
Climbs & Canyons*
Di Taylor & Tony Howard,
Cicerone Press, 2008

Treks & Climbs in Wadi Rum
Tony Howard, Cicerone Press, 2009

Field Guide to Jordan
Jarir Mani, National Press, Jordan, 2008

The Rough Guide to Jordan
Mathew Teller, Rough Guides,
next edition 2012

*Trekking & Canyoning in
the Jordanian Dead Sea Rift*
Itai Haviv, Desert Breeze Press, 2000

Climbing in Jordan
Wilf Colonna, due for publication 2012

And the books of Jane Taylor, see
www.janetaylorphotos.com/books

New routes & feedback
Anyone discovering new walks, climbs
or caves in the area or having comments
on existing routes etc should contact the
authors, see above. Details will be added
to the authors' webpage
**www.nomadstravel.co.uk/Jordan.update.
html**

Notes